WHAT MATTERS NOW

Gareth O'Callaghan is one of Ireland's most popular radio presenters, having enjoyed a successful career that has stretched across forty years. During that period he has worked for many radio stations, both at home and abroad, including RTÉ and BBC.

He also spent a number of years working as a psychotherapist in Ireland.

In 2018, Gareth took early retirement from his radio career after being diagnosed with multiple system atrophy.

He is the author of six books, including the 2003 number one bestseller *A Day Called Hope*, which documented his own personal journey through and beyond depression.

He spends much of his time these days writing and logging. He continues to challenge this awful illness through daily physical exercise, while urging others with similar debilitating conditions to do the same. He lives in Cork.

What Matters Now

A Memoir of Hope and Finding
a Way Through the Dark

GARETH O'CALLAGHAN

HACHETTE
BOOKS
IRELAND

First published in Ireland in 2021 by Hachette Books Ireland
First published in paperback in 2022

1

Cataloguing in Publication Data is available from the British Library.

ISBN 9781529333596

Typeset in Arno Pro by Bookends Publishing Services, Dublin
Printed and bound in Great Britain by Clays, Elcograf S.p.A.

Hachette Books Ireland policy is to use papers that are natural, renewable
and recyclable products and made from wood grown in sustainable forests.
The logging and manufacturing processes are expected to conform to the
environmental regulations of the country of origin.

Hachette Books Ireland
8 Castlecourt Centre
Castleknock
Dublin 15, Ireland

A division of Hachette UK Ltd
Carmelite House, 50 Victoria Embankment, EC4Y 0DZ

www.hachettebooksireland.ie

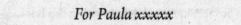

For Paula xxxxx

Some names and details within this book
have been changed to respect the privacy of individuals.

Introduction

9 OCTOBER 2019

Sunlight filled the office. It seemed like a perfect day at last; something that had been so rare in recent times. I sat close beside her, smiling nervously while saying nothing; loving that look of disbelief in her beautiful green eyes. Only four per cent of the world's population have green eyes, she would often remind me. She concentrated on the paperwork, watching for the pencilled 'x's that our solicitor, Suzanne, had tagged for her to sign her name beside. 'At last, it's here,' I could imagine her saying to herself. She was finally signing her divorce papers.

I knew she was both nervous and relieved. We both had heavy colds. We felt broken after all that had been happening, but more united than ever. Ever since the evening we'd first met in March 2015, both of us still felt in many ways like a couple of teenagers on their first date. We also felt we had aged as a result of the extreme stress and anxiety we'd been living through more recently. It was etched on our faces for all to see.

By then, that afternoon in October in our solicitor's office, we were both physically shattered; emotionally exhausted. Paula had been propping me up all this time because of this horrible illness, urging me to keep going. I just couldn't see the point at times because I felt so ill, but I didn't want to go anywhere; I just wanted to be with her.

It was hard to believe that nearly a year and a half had passed since I had received the awful news. I had never been seriously ill in my life, but now all that was changing so fast. As illnesses go, this couldn't get any more serious. Each day I swamp the discomforts with painkillers and sedatives, pills that prevent my body going into convulsive spasms; tiny tablets that relax my muscles at night so that I get a few hours of decent sleep; other pills that prevent me from acting out my dreams and hurting myself with my hands and legs or, worse still, Paula; sachets of powder that I add nightly to water and drink in order to keep my bowels working properly. Each morning as Paula massages away the chronic pain in my toes and feet with CBD oil, I insist to this gorgeous woman of mine that I am fine.

There are nights when I watch her sleeping and it washes over me that this is so unfair on her. Looking at her, I realise that her beautiful life is already predestined as a result of this horrible beast of a disease.

I couldn't have blamed her if she had made her excuses and walked away as soon as we had received the news. What she had taken on, so soon after we had met, was a front-row seat beside a guy who had a one-way ticket and was heading for the departure lounge; but she made it quite clear that she wanted nothing else, no matter how bad it might get, only to be with me all the way, through it all. I will never know where she finds the strength to be so resolutely determined.

Looking back, it felt like it had been such a long journey. It wasn't even five years since we'd met but so much had happened in that short time. I watched her carefully now as she listened to the solicitor's assurances. She was finally getting divorced, I kept thinking. It's here, at last. Our solicitor handed her the black pen one last time and pointed to the bottom of the third page. 'Sign here,' she said, indicating the blank black line.

Paula's eyes welled up. I put my arm around her shoulder and pulled her in to me tightly. Suzanne smiled. 'Well done,' she said as she got up from her chair to reach across the desk and hug Paula. For the first time in a very long time, it was as if something had shifted.

We walked out into the freezing cold October sunshine a few minutes later. We both felt as though we were finally stepping into the future we had hoped and prayed for since we had first met each other on a nightclub dancefloor in her native Cork during a radio station listeners' promotional night nearly five years earlier. Neither of us had ever experienced anything like the instant connection we both felt that evening when our eyes locked on to each other.

Our chance meeting was most definitely one of those '*Sliding Doors* moments', when a spur-of-the-moment conversation, decision or encounter completely changes the direction your life takes. Peter Howitt, director of the 1998 film *Sliding Doors*, calls it 'the cerebral flipping of the coin'. One such moment that instantly comes to mind is Princess Diana's last-minute decision to make a trip across Paris on that August night in 1997. Where would she be today if she had decided to stay in her hotel instead of getting into the back of her chauffeur-driven Mercedes S280 to return to her apartment? Another *Sliding Doors* moment has to be the 1992 signing of Eric Cantona by the then Manchester United manager, Sir Alex Ferguson. Would the team have still gone on to win four Premier League titles in five years, along with two League and FA Cup doubles without 'King Eric'?

Each and every life journey is defined by these random moments that can change the entire course of circumstances for that person, although they might have seemed inconsequential at the time. Most of the time we are too distracted by the demanding task of living to be even aware of these moments – until perhaps months or even years later when we consider how life might have turned out if, during its cerebral flip, the imaginary coin had landed the other side up.

Whenever I look back, I can identify how my own life has been shaped by such moments which have brought me to where I am now, many of which I have written about in Part One of this story. In the same way, the seemingly random events and encounters in your unique life journey account for where you are right now, as you hold this book in your hands.

On that October day, life for Paula and me was littered with unavoidable obstacles and a huge uncertainty as to what lay ahead. But we were together. We had come a long way since the warm Friday afternoon sixteen months earlier, when the same diagnosis coming from two neurologists confirmed what I had suspected for months. Could my diagnosis be yet another *Sliding Doors* moment? All I know is that this illness has been the greatest wakeup call I have ever been given. But instead of destroying me, this diagnosis has invigorated my determination to survive. It has instilled in me a belief that I can outrun the odds of a prognosis which, medical research informs me, is most definitely not in my favour.

The odds of staying alive and remaining healthy are well and truly stacked against me; my defiance is at odds with all that I have been told by the neurologists and movement disorder specialists. There are those who see my outspoken beliefs that I can 'beat this one' as bold disobedience, almost open resistance. But what is the alternative? To give in to this beast of a disease simply because neurologists tell me there's nothing I can do to prevent it from killing me? Yes, perhaps this is the *Sliding Doors* moment of all time for me, one like no other in all my sixty years. It terrifies me, but I can't just sit back and allow it to destroy me without doing everything I can possibly think of to stop it – no matter what I have been told. Am I wasting my time? Of course I'm not, because doing nothing would be akin to wasting my life – no matter how challenging the times ahead might become. When I look back, I never want to find myself saying, 'I wish I'd tried harder.' I have no doubt that I am being true to myself, and right now that's all that really matters.

Nothing can ever prepare you for bad news – very bad news; even when you get a gut feeling that you already know what's wrong long before it's finally confirmed. There's always a place somewhere inside, like a reassuring voice, that silently reminds you there's a chance it's not what you're expecting to hear. In hindsight, my hunches have usually been spot on. Call it a higher energy, or a sixth sense, but it's never let me down – even when you hope with all your will it might be wrong.

You might have spent every available opportunity on Google, engaged in your own private research that screams over and over: *You have a serious problem.* But there's always going to be that tiny space reserved somewhere in the back of your mind that keeps reminding you there's still a slim possibility you will be proved wrong.

The fuse had been lit long ago. Whatever had sparked this rare and deadly disease deep in my brain years before will probably remain a mystery to global science and its tireless researchers for many years to come. The only certainty was that it would continue in its own insidious way to rob me of my quality of life, relentlessly carving out its unique trajectory until it ran out of internal body parts that it could destroy. And then – if I managed to get that far – it would finally suffocate me.

In recent years, I'd often wondered what thoughts might cross my mind if I was ever to be given this sort of bad news, the sort that doesn't really get any worse; the 'there's-nothing-we-can-do-for-you' type of news. Of course there is worse news, such as being told that your child is dying; but thankfully that was not, and hopefully never will be, the case.

Specifically I have often thought about how I might react to being given this kind of news about my own health. Would I become hysterical? Would I curse? Could I even cope with such an irreversible diagnosis? After all, what would be the point of continuing to struggle with a life that is doomed to silent misery and eventual vegetative status; especially when you realise that the remainder of your life is inexorably moving from 'bleak' to 'bleakest'. I can't imagine the person tasked with breaking the news to me saying, '… now that's the bad news, so here's the good news …' There is no 'good news' with an illness like this. Would I start to dwell on all the things I had been putting off doing for as long as I could remember, because I was 'too busy'? Or would I even hear the words I'm being told?

I recall a close friend on a live television talk show telling those of us watching at home how he could only hear a kind of white fuzzy noise when he was being given his terminal cancer diagnosis. He explained to his host how he had watched the lips of the oncologist as they moved precisely and mouthed something, but he couldn't hear the words he was saying.

Nothing like this happened when I received the news. It was just a voice repeating much the same as I'd heard the previous day, a conversation on the radio that had jolted me into an unavoidable confrontation of the rotten indecencies of life. The doctor being interviewed was explaining how one third of the current population would have some form of a brush with cancer in their lifetime; another third would develop a neurological disorder such as Alzheimer's, Parkinson's, multiple sclerosis, or suffer a stroke; while the final third would just have to take their chances with a myriad of other horrible possibilities including heart disease, murder, self-inflicted fatal injuries, and deaths caused by dangerous recreational sports. There was also the remote possibility of getting hit by a bus. I remember thinking that it was one of the most fascinating medical interviews I had listened to in years. It was like a plot from a Stephen King novel. If I was a gambling man I would clearly choose to be in the final third for as long as I had left of this life, because it seemed to offer slightly better odds – provided you stuck to a reasonably healthy regime and retained a hopeful outlook. Of course at that time I was able to choose. But now I know that neither a healthy regime nor a hopeful outlook safeguard you whatsoever from these horrible life-threatening illnesses. Every one of us of course should lead a healthy lifestyle, if only because such a lifestyle is likely to lead to a longer, healthier life – provided the big guns of chronic illness don't spoil the plan. I know people who won medals for all sorts of sporting achievements, who stuck rigidly to training routines and fitness regimes and strict diets, who got incurable cancer, or dementia, or another serious illness. And all the time your consultant is trying his or her best, as they're delivering the diagnosis, not to dwell on the thought, 'Rather you than me, pal.'

I now belonged in the second third of the statistical pie chart. I had just been enrolled into a fringe group of random people who have 'little-known-about' or 'never-heard-of-before' diseases. I had a rare and horrible neurological illness, progressive and incurable, called multiple system atrophy (MSA for short).

I am Gareth O'Callaghan. And this is my story.

Part One

Chapter 1

A THIEF IN THE NIGHT

It was very late at night in the early weeks of 2016 when I noticed something strange happening to me for what appeared to be the first time. It had probably happened before that, but this was the point at which I could no longer ignore it: it was keeping me awake. I felt an uncomfortable itching sensation between the second and third toes on my left foot. It was so irritating that I couldn't get back to sleep. When I examined the area the next morning, I could see that I had scratched it so hard, the skin was red-raw and almost bleeding. Yet there was no sign of a bite or a splinter.

After a few weeks the persistent nightly itching became intensely annoying. It felt as though I had been bitten or stung by some sort of tiny insect that had found itself caught in the bed linen or in my sock. But it couldn't be a bite because it wasn't healing.

Sometimes it was a continuous itch. Whenever I scratched it, my toe would tremble. Other nights there would be a more concentrated twitching sensation in the second toe, as if it was resting against something that was vibrating. I couldn't stop it. I would often watch this toe as it twitched, amazed that the toes on either side were not moving. I tried sitting out on the side of the bed and pressing my toes hard onto the cold floorboards. The twitching would stop – but then within a few minutes of lying down, it would start again. This risible routine eventually became a nightly obsession while I lay in bed trying to sleep. It just didn't make any sense.

I consulted Dr Google. Itchy toes can apparently

be caused by the condition 'athlete's foot', a fungal infection otherwise known as *tinea pedis*. Someone I worked with rather sternly warned me it could be an early symptom of diabetes. Someone else I knew, who lived their life through various superstitions, told me that an itching toe was a sign that I 'would be embarking on a great journey very soon'. Meanwhile someone in my local supermarket suggested it might be caused by cheap laundry detergent. Another acquaintance told me that my twitching toe was either a sign of bad circulation or the beginning of rheumatoid arthritis. None of these possible explanations made any sense whatsoever.

I was never a great sleeper, so the slightest sensation or noise during the night would wake me. Once awake, I would lie on my back and focus on the various toe sensations. If it was the itch, I'd end up scratching it until my toes were almost raw. This eventually became a permanent feature of my nights. At first there was no pain or real discomfort involved – but that didn't last long. Sometimes the side of my left foot would ache – it would feel like a pain caused by bruising, as though I had banged it against something. I'd massage the area and the aching would normally ease. Other times I'd feel a sudden, sharp pain shooting up the side of the same foot, and then it was gone.

There were other occasions, again mostly at night, when a sharp jolt of pain would shoot up through my back muscles, or down one of my legs, causing me to jump. It felt like an electric shock. This quickly became more frequent. There were also nights when I would wake suddenly, having unconsciously hit myself in the face or the head. I had no idea why this was happening. As a light sleeper, I would become aware of the automatic jerking movement in my arm a split second before my hand would jump up and slap my head or my cheek.

I often wondered why in the mornings my teeth felt like they had moved during the night; and why they often felt so sore I couldn't clench them. The shape of my jaws would feel different when I closed my mouth. Eventually as the day wore on, my jaws would feel normal again. It turned out I had been grinding my back teeth so hard during my sleep that I had almost dislocated my jawline.

Eventually the toes on my left foot began to randomly curl inwards and then lock in a painful knot. The pain was excruciating at times. I would end up sitting on the side of the bed with my left foot straddled across my right knee as I forced the toes out of the painful cramp and massaged them straight again, only for the muscles in my foot to contract again minutes later, causing the toes to once more curl inwards.

Of course not all of these 'symptoms' were happening simultaneously; but it didn't take long until I started to worry. One morning while having a cup of coffee I made a list of the strange nocturnal activities. As I looked back over it, I began to feel very vulnerable and scared.

Looking back now, I can see a pattern of small, yet odd, symptoms developing randomly over a period of a few years prior to my diagnosis. It wasn't as if there had been someone lying beside me at night with whom I could share these strange moments as I was experiencing them. I had been living on my own, renting a small but comfortable apartment in Dublin, in a beautiful location close to the Royal Canal. Paula lived in Cork, one hundred and fifty miles away. There were many nights I wanted to call her to chat about these bizarre sensations, but I knew she worked long days in her own job and needed her rest. I didn't want to worry her. I knew she was going through a difficult time herself.

It's often the little things that catch a woman's attention – things that men either ignore or fail to notice. What I didn't know was that by that time Paula was already extremely worried about what was happening to me. She had noticed tremors in both of my hands, but decided against saying anything. She knew I had issues with anxiety and just put these tremors down to stress.

As time passed I began to notice, as part of my nightly observations, that my feet felt somehow different. My left foot felt awkward and inactive compared to my right foot, which seemed slightly livelier and more flexible and mobile. The toes on my right foot moved quickly, whereas everything about my left foot seemed like an effort. Even my walking pattern was changing. My left foot seemed slower to respond, as though it was operating from a different set of instructions to the right foot.

There was also a problem with night sweats. Sometimes I would wake up on a cold night lying in bed linen that was soaking wet. It was so bad on some occasions, my initial reaction was that I must have wet the bed. The profuse sweating usually happened on those cold nights, which made no sense to me whatsoever. There were times when I would put my socks back on in an effort to get heat into my toes, even though the rest of my body felt warm. And yet on warmer, humid nights, I faced the opposite problem and seemed physically incapable of sweating; I'd lie there without any bedclothes covering me, wishing I could cool down. My brain would feel as though it was overheating, with my heart pounding like a hammer in my chest, and not a single bead of sweat breaking anywhere on my body – except for my lower back, which would feel saturated.

I was also losing count of the nights I woke up dizzy and gasping for breath, as if I had stopped breathing and had suddenly restarted just as I felt I was about to suffocate. Sometimes I would wake with a parched mouth, so dry I couldn't swallow. My tongue would feel like a dry sponge or sandpaper. On other nights I'd wake to find I had been drooling so badly that the pillow was soaked. More often now, I was being woken by a ferocious jerk that would shoot through one of my legs, or down my back, or across my shoulders. These jerks (known as myoclonic jerks) were both sporadic and spasmodic, like the sensation of a sharp electric shock, and they were painful enough to leave me wide awake and worried. As more time went by, the toes of my left foot began to regularly feel completely numb, even during the warmer summer weather. It didn't take long until the toes on my right foot followed suit.

All of this was part of a progressive pattern that eventually started to drag me downhill. At times I lost the will to live – everything was becoming such a struggle. I was doing my best to convince myself that all these physical problems were being caused by stress and anxiety. At that time I was presenting a five-hour-long show, five days a week, as well as an early Sunday morning show on Classic Hits, a radio station I had been working for since the day it first came on air in 2009. There was a huge amount of preparation required for each of the shows, and then there was the administrative work involved in preparing the programme for the following day. My average radio day at the station started around 11 a.m., and often continued until 9 p.m., many evenings during the week. And then there were the Sunday shows. While it was a dream job in many ways, it was also highly stressful; and the simple fact was that I had very little time off to relax and unwind.

The radio station probably couldn't have chosen a worse time for its official launch in 2009. Within weeks the country's economy was spiralling into a deep and dark recession, one of the worst in living memory. Months after its first broadcast, the station was in financial trouble. By the end of its first year it was taking every opportunity to pull back on what it was spending. Staff were being let go, and those who remained took substantial pay cuts. I had my wages cut on two occasions in a short space of time which left me quickly falling into debt. As a self-employed sole trader I was responsible at the end of each tax year for paying the income tax owed from the previous year but, because my wages were now significantly lower, my bank account quickly ran out of money. I was warned by close friends that this was inevitable. My marriage had ended in late 2005 and I had moved into temporary accommodation nearby. I had been advised to sell the family home, and that would alleviate all of the debts owed, but I had told my daughters that I would rather find myself homeless than leave them in a position where they might find themselves looking for somewhere else to live.

Financial pressure and debt ate away at my life for years. I seemed to be permanently struggling to find money, even for the simple things like a weekend away, or gifts for birthdays and Christmas. That nagging reminder that I owed money overshadowed everything. I was constantly anxious that I wouldn't have enough to pay monthly rent and bills. I had little if any money to spend on myself. I just couldn't get away from it.

Outside of my long hours on the radio, everything eventually seemed overshadowed by a general lack of interest. Apathy had set in; I just didn't care. I felt exhausted after doing the simplest things, like changing the kitchen bin, or walking the two flights of stairs from the main door to my apartment on the first floor. Even after a short walk, I found myself needing to sit down just to catch my breath. I was low on energy and tired all the time. My life was stuck in some timeless rut, where days just morphed into weeks. It was as though I was coming down with a really bad cold, never moving past that initial stage where you feel just rotten and the temptation to climb back into bed is always there.

Something was dying deep inside my brain, zapping my life force. This is exactly how it felt. By the start of 2015, I was worried for my health, deeply worried, but what could I do? My finances were spiralling out of control. That tiny voice deep inside was telling me I was heading for a fall. It would only be a matter of time. Something was going to happen to me if I didn't stop this way of living. But how could I stop? I needed money to stop. I had no money. I had to keep earning in order to keep paying: Catch 22. I was like a gerbil on a wheel that just keeps on spinning around and around.

I knew that my passion and enthusiasm for my radio work was slowly slipping away from me. It was a passion I had thrived on from a young age and was very proud of; an enthusiasm that I thought would continue to steer my career for at least another ten years. I was now just going through the motions. Most mornings I woke with an intense dread and loathing for the day ahead, so overwhelming at times that it made no sense to me. It had become the same routine for at least a year, maybe more. Every day I would drag myself out of bed, exhausted and agitated, having been awake since before five – or whenever the twitching and itching, or the muscular jerks, had woken me. There were mornings I just didn't have the energy to get up or go to work. On those mornings I would often just text the programme director, explain that I was unwell, and then turn over and go back to sleep. On the days I wasn't working, I found it slightly easier to relax; and at weekends when Paula was around, having travelled from Cork to Dublin to stay with me, things seemed very different and far more manageable.

Although there were times I felt like I was heading for either a major breakdown or a massive heart attack, I knew I had to keep going. I needed money –

not just to pay the bills but because I was still paying amounts off the money I owed. On one occasion in December 2015, my debit card failed to work in a local ATM machine close to my apartment. I thought maybe the card had been damaged so I dropped in to the closest bank branch that morning to sort it out.

After checking her computer screen, I was told politely by the teller that someone would come out to chat with me shortly and if I could step aside from the queue at the counter. I knew this couldn't be good news. My heart sank even further as I waited the best part of half an hour before one of the branch managers approached me. The look on her face did nothing for my deflated spirit. She informed me in a hushed voice that an attachment order had been placed on my bank account and that I was not permitted to access the money in it under any circumstances. This was money I needed in order to pay my bills, to buy Christmas gifts, to buy food. As I left the bank that morning, it started to snow. I looked down at my shoes and asked them to carry me home. I felt so weak that I thought I would collapse. I was mortified.

I cried as I walked towards the railway station,

realising as I looked up at the heavy, grey, snowy sky that I didn't even have enough coins in my pockets to pay for dinner. I decided to walk the five miles home, opting for a microwave dinner from my local supermarket instead of spending the money on a train ticket.

I passed a young man sitting in a doorway holding an empty paper coffee cup. I imagined all of a sudden that it was me in the doorway. I kept walking. I thought to myself that I could just disappear that day. I could step out of the rat race right now if I really wanted to. I could find a bed in a homeless shelter. I had no money – *no money*! I was halfway home. Something kept telling me that I would be fine if I could just get inside my hall door and close it behind me. I would be safe there. Right then, as I crossed busy streets, with the festive lights hanging overhead, and the distant husky voice of a street busker singing 'Fairytale of New York', I was terrified. The word unhinged comes to mind. I wanted to be held, to be told that everything was going to be okay. I remember looking at the sky and begging for someone to send me some kind of sign, that it would all be sorted and I would have money.

I counted at least five people begging on the city streets that morning. Was it because I had no money that I noticed them? The snow turned to heavy rain, and it poured for almost an hour. I was soaked to the skin by the time I reached home. I woke the following morning with the worst flu I have ever experienced in my life. I couldn't move far from my bed for almost four days. The weather was too unpredictable, and the roads too treacherous, for Paula to travel from Cork.

The stress was becoming unbearable, but I kept it hidden – or so I thought. Then, out of nowhere came a glimmer of hope. While searching the kitchen drawers for some loose change, I found my credit union book which I hadn't used for years. I had €157 in my account. It wasn't a lot but at least I could stock up the fridge. Eventually the situation was resolved thanks in no small way to Paula, who managed to secure a loan for me, and to the generosity of my brother and my parents.

Still, I felt as though I was slipping back into a depression that I hadn't experienced since the nineties. It seemed very recognisable, very real. I frequently forgot where I had put my keys, and it annoyed me that I couldn't remember passwords on my PC, or my bank account number or various user IDs. But then, maybe minutes or even hours later, I would suddenly be able to recall them. At one point I also entertained the terrifying notion that I might be in the early stages of dementia.

When I mentioned my fears to a doctor, he reassured me that it wasn't Alzheimer's disease, or any other type of dementia. 'Someone with Alzheimer's,' he told me, 'doesn't just forget where they left their keys; someone with Alzheimer's doesn't know what keys are for.' I found this explanation to be simplistic and rather chilling; but at a time when I felt as though my life was in freefall, it came as a huge relief to be told by my doctor that I didn't have one of the worst illnesses imaginable. However, these reassurances from him still didn't stop me from turning to the internet.

I had been told about a test that is used to assess whether or not a patient might have a form of dementia. I think it's called the 'clock test', which I duly carried out myself. Firstly I had to draw a large circle on a blank sheet of A4 paper; I used a saucer to draw the circle. Then, imagining the circle was the face of a blank clock, I had to draw clock hands to show the time at 15.20; I was to do this as quickly as possible. I was able to complete this task almost instantly. I sat back in my chair and breathed a huge sigh of relief. I shut down the laptop and went to bed. Of course, I was completely overlooking the fact that I couldn't do the test properly and accurately unless I was in the presence of a doctor. For the test to be accurate, he or she would have to choose the time, not me! Someone with signs of dementia, seemingly, may find this test very challenging. All the patient can see is a blank circle. When the doctor asks them to show the time 10 minutes after 11 (which is a time many doctors choose to use for this test), my understanding is that it's the combination of delay and frustration that alerts the doctor or specialist to the likelihood of a dementia issue.

Although I was temporarily reassured by my doctor's words and my clock test, I continued to have a very clear sense that there was something wrong with me health-wise, and that it was slowly getting worse. One night I woke up in a fit of coughing. I couldn't catch my breath. I eased myself out onto the side of the bed and straightened my back. I realised immediately that I was having a full-blown asthma attack – something I hadn't experienced since I'd given up smoking eighteen years before. I started to pull out drawers and look inside kitchen presses, searching for an old Ventolin inhaler that I knew I had put away somewhere for safe keeping; somewhere so safe that I couldn't now find it! I eventually located it, checked the expiry date ... BBE 10/2010. The inhaler was out of date.

My sense of panic was making the asthma worse. I felt as though I was slowly choking. The inhaler might still work. I couldn't get it into my mouth fast enough. I took the protective cover off the mouthpiece and shook the tube vigorously, placed it between my lips and fired three shots. I breathed in deeply and felt the cool spray fill my lungs. Within seconds I could feel the relief.

As anyone with asthma will tell you, an asthma attack is both terrifying, because it mostly occurs unexpectedly, and physically exhausting. I went back to bed, lay down and closed my eyes. I could feel my heart pounding so hard that the headboard was tapping against the wall almost in time to the rapid heartbeats. It seemed that my asthma had returned, and it didn't take long for my doctor to confirm it. Apparently it's not uncommon for asthma to occur in youth, then to disappear, and later to recur in middle age. I'd been having more upper respiratory viral infections than usual, and this can cause the dormant asthma to rear its nasty head again, which is precisely what happened in late 2016.

Around this time I was revisited by another problem I thought I'd dealt with and put behind me years before. After thirty years of relief from it, my obsessive compulsive disorder (OCD) had become unmanageable again – through the roof in fact. It was taking me the best part of an hour to lock up and leave my apartment each day before I went to work, as I made myself check the taps in the kitchen and bathroom; then all of the light switches, the immersion, the central heating, the windows, the plug sockets – all of them, at least five times; and finally the front door lock. It was usually that damn door lock that I got 'stuck' on. I often returned back up the stairs to check it 'just five more times while I counted to nine'. Most days I would phone Paula as I was about to leave for work in an effort to distract myself from the punishing, frustrating ritual that felt as though it was slowly destroying me.

Most people have very mild OCD, most likely without even being aware of it. For them it's not a disorder, nor is it an overwhelming distraction. It's more of an extra-cautious sense of reassurance for them when, after locking the front door, they check the handle three times; or they might find a certain kind of inner comfort in their habit of arranging the contents of the fridge in a certain way.

However, if you check the door handle and then you're compelled to go back to it again and again, checking each time until you're in danger of physically breaking it, then you have a form of OCD that is interfering with your life on a number of levels. In the same way, if placing the contents of the fridge in a particular order becomes a daily ritual so rigid that you refuse to let anyone else near the fridge, then your habit might be considered to be intrusive, in that it is limiting your freedom to live life like most other people do.

When OCD reaches serious levels of disrupting your peace of mind and your ability to resist the demons, it can threaten to take over your life and deprive you of your freedom. It controls you. It torments you and haunts you. It drives you beyond your ability to control it. When it is extreme, the mind becomes distracted by unmanageable habits and rituals that you feel the overwhelming need to carry out meticulously, and then to repeat each one over and over again.

Such behaviour becomes compulsive and it's almost always accompanied by recurring thoughts that you habitually dwell on, or obsess over. You might ruminate that if the compulsions are not carried out in a certain precise and ritualistic way, something terrible is going to happen to someone you love, or a fire might start, or your apartment might be broken into. Of course nothing is going to happen to anyone you love if you don't perform the rituals. There won't be any fire, or burglary, because it's simply a mind game. But for those who have to endure life at the extreme end of the OCD scale every day, it's far from a game that they are playing. It can become a matter of life or death; it's a never-ending nightmare that can deprive you of your ability to live freely.

Now, at the beginning of 2017, my mind seemed to be turning against me again. It was the same thing every morning as I struggled with the compulsive madness of my rituals before I could leave for work. On the other end of the line, Paula would urge me to keep moving. I'd hold the phone to my ear so I could hear her reassuring voice, as I checked each appliance, walking from room to room, counting to nine three times and then blinking twice while focusing on whatever it was I was checking. If I lost count at any stage, everything went back to zero and the checking would have to commence all over again.

On one occasion, I became 'stuck'. I physically couldn't move my feet: it was as though they were frozen to the wooden floor. This would prove significant in later clinical tests.

'My feet won't move,' I said to Paula.

There was silence.

I said it again. 'My feet won't move. They're stuck.'

'Where are they stuck?' I could hear the concern in her voice. 'I don't know what you mean.'

Then, just as though nothing had happened, my feet shuffled and moved. I wriggled my toes. Despite a feeling of dull heaviness around my ankles, my feet seemed to be fine again. Then I became aware of the drool again at the side of my mouth. I wiped it with a tissue. That day I was late for my train.

On another occasion – there were many – after getting completely exasperated somewhere in my daily ritual, I just gave up. Mentally broken and physically exhausted, I sat down and cried. I was convinced that my OCD was finally driving me insane. That day I didn't go to work.

This was the pattern of my life behind closed doors. It had become a daily curse; it was as though I was somehow punishing myself. However, on the days when Paula was physically with me, it was a very different story. If on a scale of one to ten my daily levels of OCD regularly sky-rocketed to around an eight, they dropped way back to a very manageable two at weekends, whenever Paula was around.

This was not part of the natural ageing process. I was fifty-six years of age. My mind still felt strong, my mental faculties appeared to be razor-sharp, despite my fears of dementia. However, I just knew I was becoming more separated from the life I had been familiar with, as if something deep inside my head was becoming unhinged. Something just wasn't right, and whatever it was, it seemed to be getting worse.

Yet each day, as I closed my front door behind me and walked the short distance to the railway station, I was no different from your average commuter on his way to work. There were no visible signs of the anxiety and deep unease that were eating me up inside. Outwardly I appeared to be mechanically functional. I was maintaining some semblance of normality to the outside world. Or so I thought.

All that changed one morning, not long after I had arrived into work. By now it was towards the end of 2017. I had just filled a mug with hot coffee when I dropped it, scalding my leg and my right foot. Later that day, after I had treated the burns on my legs and toes, I slowly realised that my left hand was now behaving like my left foot. It was as though something

– whatever it was – was spreading up the left side of my body. I had held the mug like I usually did as I filled it from the kettle; but it was as though my hand had suddenly lost all its power to grip the mug firmly. It just flopped lifelessly, dropping the mug on the spot. There was no warning. Then, almost as though nothing had happened, my left hand felt normal again, except for a noticeable twitch, which I put down to the fright I got and the pain of a scalded foot.

On further investigation later that day, however, I realised that what I had passed off as normal was far from that. My left hand had become noticeably weaker than my right hand. I could no longer squeeze it shut as quickly as my right. It felt clumsy. I could detect a dull pain in the third and fourth fingers. That seemed new. I'm right-handed mostly, but this seemed more than just strange. Now I was more worried than ever before. That same evening, I carefully examined both hands. I straightened them and held them out in front of me as I stood in the kitchen. That was when I noticed they were both twitching. Once more, I put it down to stress, considering my anxiety levels were at an all-time high at that point.

There were other incidents that I could no longer put down to being random accidents. Early one morning in December 2017 after taking a shower, I turned and fell out over the side of the bath. Thankfully I grabbed hold of the bath as I was falling – otherwise my head would have hit the tiled floor. If that had happened, I might not be sitting here writing about it today.

On another occasion – again I had just arrived in work – I tripped over a leather couch just inside the main door of the office. I knew it was there; it had always been there – it was where guests sat and waited before being brought to the studio for interviews. I regularly sat on it myself while eating my lunch. Every morning as I arrived at work I would automatically walk around this long black leather couch, as part of a subconscious routine. It had registered with that region in my brain that deals with routines, and retains important information on simple things and learned behaviours that you do every day, things you just take for granted so you don't have to keep learning them all afresh every time.

I knew for certain now that something was

seriously wrong in my brain. I was terrified. And what if everyone thought I had been drinking before my radio show?

On that particular day, however, it was as if I had never seen the couch before, so I fell over it. But I did know it was there; my eyes could see it. But for some unknown reason, the neurons failed to send the signal from my brain: 'You are approaching the couch. Veer to the left right now!' And so even though I could see it, I fell over it. The part of my brain that was responsible for carrying out the complex but automatic coordination of simple, everyday movements throughout my body had not responded in time. Or perhaps it had failed completely to respond?

A small group stood around me, with concerned faces. One of them helped me back onto my feet. And then I heard the question. 'Have you been drinking?' I laughed it off. Of course it was meant as a joke, but there was nothing funny about what was happening to me, whatever it was. Not only was I mortified, I was now also experiencing a fear of the unknown.

Later that evening, on the train journey home, I

kept replaying the earlier couch scene over and over in my head. After what must have been almost two years of trying to downplay my symptoms, I had to accept that there was something wrong with me. What I didn't realise was that it was far more serious than I could ever have imagined.

Chapter 2

MY DOCTOR'S OFFICE

Sunshine has always made me feel so much better. Even on the days when I might be feeling low, the presence of strong, warm sunlight can still find its way deep inside me, sparking a joy and an appreciation for the warmth it helps me to feel. I remember that Tuesday morning, 19 February 2018, was cold and sunny, a perfect early spring day with those beautiful high, blue skies.

I had made an appointment to see my doctor the previous day. When his secretary asked what was wrong with me, I told her I didn't know. She booked me in for a 10.30 a.m. consultation. Even though he was my doctor, I was nervous at the prospect of sitting in front of a man who for many years I'd considered a close friend, discussing symptoms that were by now affecting me in all sorts of strange and embarrassing ways.

It had all come to a head almost six weeks before in January during my radio show, while I was flicking through an old copy of the *Irish Daily Mail* that had been left lying around in the studio. It was the face I recognised first; David 'Kid' Jensen was his name. Listeners to Radio Luxembourg back in the seventies will remember his rich voice and Canadian accent. He had been one of the reasons why I wanted my own radio show as soon as I left school. I loved his shows, and his smooth, natural style of presentation. The newspaper article was a double-page spread. The headline made my jaw drop: '"I've been living with Parkinson's for five years", says Kid Jensen.' I read the article as quickly as I could. My mouth was parched dry. My fingers were trembling as I held open the newspaper in front of me. And then I read the words: 'Parkinson's affects the central nervous system and the most obvious early signs are shaking as well as other problems with motor functions.' That was when I put the paper down and realised I needed to have a talk with my doctor.

Typically, I found excuses to delay calling him. I had no doubt whatsoever that I had some sort of illness, but I was terrified of the consequence of a full medical examination. Part of me just didn't want to know what was wrong, and there was definitely something seriously wrong. Distraction works wonderfully for procrastination, so I allowed myself to focus on other things and didn't make the call for six weeks after reading that article. During that time, though, I couldn't get the newspaper interview out of my head. I kept thinking that if I replaced David Jensen's name with mine, the article could just as easily have been written about me.

I needed help. My life was falling apart. Or was it? I was trying to hide what was happening to me from everyone who knew me. Yet part of me was also relieved that now, hopefully, I would finally find out what was wrong with me. But could it be cured? What if it was severe depression? I might have to go back on the heavy-duty antidepressants I took for almost two years back in the late nineties. They were called Dosulepin, sometimes better known as Prothiaden, from a group of medicines known as tricyclic antidepressants. I found the side effects were unpleasant, including extreme tiredness, a dry mouth, and weight gain. I am often asked to this day if they worked for me, and I answer yes and no: they helped to alleviate the awful sense of foreboding that accompanied my depression, but there was a price to pay, namely the side effects. As one psychiatrist asked me, 'Would you prefer severe depression, or no depression with a few manageable side effects?' It was a ridiculous question, considering that no one knows why antidepressants work for some people, but not for others. In fact, while doctors and scientists know a little about what these drugs do inside our brains, they still don't know how much of the effects are placebo and how much are caused by the actual drug. I wanted to avoid taking antidepressants if possible, but if they helped me I was willing to give them another go.

What if it was very bad news? And if it was, would I be better off not knowing? That's ridiculous, I told myself; you can only hope to cure it if you know what it is. As I walked towards the surgery in the sunshine, I was playing a game of twenty questions with myself. I had been putting off this moment for too long.

It would take me forty-five minutes to comfortably walk the two miles from my apartment to the doctor's surgery. The exercise would do me good, I told myself. I listened to some songs on my phone as a distraction. It didn't work. Nothing would take my mind off all the possible outcomes of the appointment. Maybe it's just stress, I reassured myself.

I was getting to play my favourite songs every day of the week on one of the most popular radio shows in the entire country. Who could ever get bored of doing that? I never thought I would tire of something so special that I had loved doing for most of my life. This was just one of the many issues that I couldn't make any sense of that morning as I arrived at the surgery.

I am grateful that I have a brilliant GP. He is kind, empathic and insightful. He takes his time with me and listens to what I need to say. He reassures me and, most importantly, he respects and values my opinions. In 2003 I wrote *A Day Called Hope*, which was the story of that period of my life when I suffered from severe depression during the 1990s. I specifically said in my book that if you can't call your doctor by his first name and you don't feel comfortable whenever you find the need to visit him, then you should get yourself another doctor.

When I sat down in front of Michael that Tuesday morning, I was worried. My heart was galloping, my legs were restless, and my hands were shaking. I could tell he was taking it all in, even before I had a chance to explain.

'How are you?' he asked.

'Not great.' It was always going to be my reply on that particular day.

During the forty minutes I spent in my doctor's office, he performed a series of physical and clinical tests on my arms, legs, hands, neck, abdomen, eyes and ears. He checked my balance, asking me to walk across the office and back a few times. Referring to his notes, he reminded me of previous visits when I'd had a variety of ailments checked out.

That morning he asked me to list as many symptoms as I could recall from the months prior to making this appointment. Thankfully I had written them down: severe neck and shoulder pain that often would leave me almost paralysed with its chronic intensity ('coat-hanger pain' as it's known because of the shape of the pain line from deep within the back of the neck, out across the backs of the shoulders and then forming in a straight line across the cervical spine towards the top of the back); dizziness (which became so severe on a number of occasions I almost fainted); having to visit the bathroom regularly during the night (too regularly on some nights); bladder retention and occasional leakage (very embarrassing, depending on where I was when it happened); severe constipation (often lasting days) followed by chronic diarrhoea where I might have less than a minute's notice to get to a bathroom. Also:

dropping things and tripping; dragging my left foot occasionally; sleep apnoea; insomnia; sudden bouts of overwhelming fatigue and physical weakness; uncontrollable shaking which would start without warning; sporadic and painful jerks throughout my body; nightmares; night wheezing; night sweats as though my body was no longer able to regulate its own temperature.

I came to the end of the list. Michael concentrated on the screen in front of him as he typed my information into his computer. When he had finished, he closed his hands and placed them under his nose, and focused intensely on the screen, which reflected in his glasses. He breathed a long sigh. I gathered there was a process of elimination taking place. Something inside was telling me this was not going to end favourably.

Earlier that morning as I walked to the surgery, Paula had called me from work to wish me all the best, and to reassure me that whatever had been causing this physical misery over the previous months (and long before that) would be resolved in the coming weeks, now that I was laying it out in front of my doctor. She told me on many occasions – and she was right – that I was allowing my life to be slowly destroyed by chronic stress and anxiety, brought on mainly by financial issues and by the relentless pressures of work.

I am a permanent worrier. That in itself causes its own inbuilt set of problems. I worry about the amount of things I am constantly worrying about. I would be worried if I wasn't worrying. I worry when other people are worried. I worry because I'm worrying so much. Worrying is a vicious circle, and that can be very worrying!

'I don't believe you have an illness,' Paula had said during a brief conversation earlier that morning. 'But I do think you are so stressed out, you could be making yourself sick.' She had a point. Then she asked, 'What do you think it is?'

I hadn't told her about the David 'Kid' Jensen article I had read at work some weeks earlier. I had even read it again that morning. To be honest, by that stage, I had read it dozens of times. I waited a moment before answering. 'I think I have Parkinson's.'

'You don't have Parkinson's!' She sounded

frustrated now. I was sorry that I had made her feel this way. We were dealing with a lot of personal shit in our own individual lives at that stage, and now here we were trying to make sense of this weird behaviour that my body was randomly throwing at me. 'I'm not going to listen to this,' she said quite abruptly. 'Call me when you get out. I love you.' She suddenly hung up on me. It was most unlike her. But maybe she was right. Maybe I was just stupidly worrying about something I had allowed myself to create in my head over time?

I sat staring at my doctor. He looked concerned. He mumbled something as he looked up at me from his computer. 'Par–kin–son ... ism,' he said softly but determinedly, drawing out the word fully, almost as though he was searching through the notes he had written for something I had missed. He looked back down again at what he had been writing.

'Is it Parkinson's disease?' I asked nervously, the worry evident in my voice.

He shook his head. 'It has symptoms that are sometimes similar to idiopathic Parkinson's disease ... but it's not Parkinson's.' He seemed to stall, as if to check back over what he had been typing. 'Have you ever heard of Parkinsonism?'

'No,' I replied. 'Is it like Parkinson's?' I had spent the previous afternoon googling various medical websites about the possibility that I might have Parkinson's, but this was a new one on me.

He looked back at the screen again. He shook his head slowly while adjusting his glasses. He seemed to be searching for the most appropriate words. He explained to me that Parkinsonism is a collective term for a number of conditions that can initially mimic some of the symptoms of Parkinson's ... but it's not Parkinson's, he said, 'if that makes sense'.

It didn't.

'It's a term used for a group of neurological disorders that cause problems, like tremors and stiffness, and other symptoms that are somewhat similar to what you'd see with Parkinson's ... at the start, that is.'

'But it's not Parkinson's,' I added.

He shook his head. 'It doesn't look like it. But I'm not a neurologist.'

There was a lag in the conversation, and a sense

now that we were looking at something that required a more extensive investigation that I detected was beyond his medical jurisdiction.

'Is it serious?' I asked. Was he telling me I was seriously ill? I had never heard of Parkinsonism. Was it curable? I knew that Parkinson's disease was incurable, but I had always thought that it was a disorder that developed slowly; that you were into your sixties before you were diagnosed, and that someone with Parkinson's could continue to live a reasonably healthy, independent life well into much older age.

He looked back at the notes. I watched his eyes move across the computer screen. 'I need you to see a neurologist,' he said.

Chapter 3

THOSE SPECIAL MORNINGS

For almost fifteen years, including those when I worked for Classic Hits, I visited my parents most mornings during the week on my way in to the radio station. I would call to the house around eleven, and the three of us would sit around the kitchen table chatting about the day's news and reminiscing on old times. We would eat slices of toast and lose track of how many cups of tea we went through until it was time for me to head off and catch my train to work.

These were mornings I loved so dearly for many years and will treasure forever.

This was the house I called home for all of my childhood, up until the weekend I moved to England when I was twenty-three. It was a very happy home, growing up alongside my younger brother and sister, David and Amy. It was situated cosily in a small, quiet cul-de-sac, just off the busy Navan Road in Dublin, and was a place where neighbours always looked out for each other and childhood friendships were made that would last a lifetime.

Neither of my parents had any idea why I had visited my doctor that morning, so I expected they would both be deeply shocked when I explained the news to them. I didn't want to frighten them, even though I was feeling a sense of unease and uncertainty about the future deep down inside. I was a nervous wreck that morning, to be honest. I wasn't even sure how I was going to explain it to them.

The moment I sat down at the kitchen table I could tell by the uncomfortable silence that there was something else going on apart from my own news, which I hadn't even broken to them yet.

'How did you get on?' my mother asked. She poured some tea into a mug and placed it in front of me.

'I got some bad news,' I said, trying to keep my tone as cheerful and as hopeful as I could. 'The doctor thinks I have some type of Parkinson's. I have to go to see a neurologist whenever I can get an appointment.'

Silence in the kitchen.

I wasn't sure what to say next. 'He explained to me that there are different conditions' – I didn't want to use the word 'diseases' – 'that can mimic Parkinson's, and then they go a different direction and, like, become a different condition.' I decided I'd said enough. I could see they were both clearly shocked and a little confused by what I was saying. I know I would be too, if one of my own children called me to tell me they had an incurable illness.

'I'm so sorry to hear that,' my dad said quietly. He sat to the left of me, where he always sat every morning during our conversations. I looked across at him and patted his arm. He was different that morning, in a number of ways. Apart from eating less and sleeping more, I'd noticed more subtle changes in him lately – a tendency to chat less, and a sadness that wasn't in keeping with his upbeat nature. Perhaps I just assumed it was all part of the ageing process. He was eighty-nine, and we were all looking forward to his ninetieth birthday celebrations in August.

'We were also at the doctor this morning,' my mother said, 'weren't we, Joe?' It was as if she wanted my dad to take up the conversation now and tell me more. This was serious. There was something wrong here; I could sense it. I had always dreaded the day that either one of my parents would become seriously ill. The older they got, the more likely it became. I realised I was about to hear some more bad news.

'I had to just get a blood test done. That's all,' he said.

My father had been feeling unwell for the past month or so. He had been sleeping a lot later into the mornings than usual, delaying his daily routine of coming downstairs for his porridge and tea to when he heard me arriving at the front door, or my mother returning home from mass in our local church. He had lost quite a lot of weight and wasn't eating as heartily as he usually would. He mentioned to me on a couple of those mornings that he had a lot of heartburn around his chest and that it felt uncomfortable to eat.

I'd noticed in recent weeks that he hadn't been eating at all whenever we sat together in the mornings. And instead of his usual two or three full mugs of tea, he was now taking an hour to finish just the one. His face looked gaunt and sad. He'd even stopped having his favourite red wine, which he usually enjoyed a couple of glasses of with his dinner in the evenings.

My dad had developed macular degeneration many years previously – a medical condition which can result in blurred or no vision in the centre of the visual field if it's not caught in time. Dad's damage to the macula of the retina of his eyes was so severe he was now almost blind. While he found it very frustrating, he never showed it. However, I knew that it had broken his heart to have to give up his favourite pastime of singing in a number of Dublin choirs because he could no longer read music. Even his beloved newspaper crosswords had eventually become impossible to manage.

Despite all the challenges that came with increasingly impaired vision and the prospect of total blindness, Dad always remained positive and spirited throughout his ordeal. He loved good stories and laughed heartily at jokes, the bolder the better. Even though he outlived all of his close friends, he never appeared down or depressed. He would mention occasionally that he missed their company, but he was closest to my mother.

As his vision deteriorated, he adjusted as cheerfully as he could to the ongoing challenge; taking his daily walk most afternoons in the Phoenix Park arm in arm with my mother, and enjoying their time in the evenings sharing the crosswords, and listening to classical music on his favourite radio station, Lyric FM. There was only one exception to his choice of radio listening, and that was when I was on air. He always made a point of making sure my mother had my frequency tuned in on their car radio so they could listen in to my show during their afternoon drives to and from the park.

My parents spent virtually all their time together. Mam was Dad's fulltime carer but it never seemed like a difficult chore to her. There was always a great sense of sharing between them, and you just knew whenever you saw them together that they loved each other so much. Dad used to always call my mother his soulmate.

But his form had changed in the weeks leading up to the CBC (complete blood count) he underwent that morning. It was clear to me that Dad knew something was wrong, and that it was only a matter of time before something would give.

Chapter 4

MUSIC WAS MY FIRST LOVE:
EARLY YEARS

Often I am asked what I loved most about being on radio down through the years. Without doubt, it was the connection I had with my listeners, many of whom had been listening to me since the late seventies and early eighties. Radio is such a unique medium. It is theatre of the mind. It is one to one, a presenter and a listener; and when you add to that bond the music that your listener loves and can relate to, you have created a winning formula.

In October 1920, KDKA in Pittsburgh, Pennsylvania received its licence and went on air as the first US-licensed commercial broadcasting station on 2 November that year, to broadcast the presidential election results. This was the first election to be held after the end of the First World War. Republican Senator Warren G. Harding of Ohio defeated Democratic Governor James M. Cox, also from Ohio.

As I write this, exactly one hundred years later to the precise day, I am sitting in my small office listening to Democratic nominee Joe Biden slogging it out against the Republican President Donald Trump. This important anniversary will no doubt go unnoticed, most likely due to the speed at which radio and modern media, and people's insatiable need to be entertained instantly, moves from one topic to another. The competition for the ears of listeners is fierce today, more so than ever before.

One hundred years ago millions of Americans were glued to their old homemade radio sets to listen to

KDKA – whose reception quality was almost inaudible depending on what type of device you were using – until the final votes were counted between these little-known candidates from the swing state of Ohio. It was a fascinating contest that gripped the imaginations of an entire nation, considering neither of the two candidates was president at the time of the election. The Democratic president, Woodrow Wilson, was hoping for a third term but his party leaders believed he was by then neither popular enough nor well enough for them to re-nominate him. Former president Theodore Roosevelt was the Republicans' choice for nomination but he died the year before the election without leaving an heir to his legacy. One can only imagine what voters throughout the United States must have been thinking when you consider that if you didn't live in the state of Ohio, it's most likely you would never have heard of either of these two men.

KDKA was the only medium, apart from the traditional newsreels, that gave an enormous electorate an insight into the lives of the two candidates. There was no television as we know it today, no mobile phones, no social media, in fact no other way for people to discuss the strengths and weaknesses of these two relative strangers, who both wanted to be the most influential person in the Western world. It's also worth noting that millions of women would be permitted to vote for the first time in the nation's history in this classic election.

The most popular entertainer in America at the time, Al Jolson, swayed the nation for Harding, singing songs on the radio that compared him to one of the most popular Republican presidents of all time, Abraham Lincoln. Harding won the election in a massive landslide, pulling more than seven million more votes than Cox. While Cox travelled twenty-two thousand miles making over four hundred speeches, Harding adopted the tactic of conducting a front-porch campaign, where he literally sat in a wicker chair in his front porch in Marion, Ohio, drawing on all the clichés he could think of, while urging a 'return to normalcy' for the nation after the hardships of the world war, while the journalists sat in his garden taking notes.

After a horrendous and bloody war that had

claimed the lives of thousands of Americans, leaving thousands more seriously ill and injured, the nation just wanted to be normal again. Harding had never been heard of outside of Ohio before 1920. Now he was the president of the United States, thanks mainly to the power of music and the luring persuasion of normalcy.

Harding was not America's most popular president, by a long shot, considering his term was rocked by scandals; but it's probably worth mentioning that he invented what has become an international fixation, namely the presidential celebrity endorsement. Six hundred thousand people visited the small town of Marion, Ohio, during the campaign to listen to Harding's front porch speeches about normalcy, the importance of integrity and the family home and Mama's sweet apple pie; in fact nothing of political importance. Politics is short-lived, whereas normalcy is always sought after, no matter what generation we look back on. In the one hundred years since Harding became president, another fact remains intact: people tire quickly of politics, but they never get tired of a great celebrity.

For Harding and his wife Florence Kling, and his genius adviser, advertising veteran Albert Lasker, this campaign had nothing to do with speeches; it was all about celebrities, show business and A-listers. Al Jolson was the hottest ticket in 1920s America. He was the star of Broadway, soon to be the first human being ever to speak in a movie, and was all over the newsreels. The day Al Jolson stood on Harding's front porch and sang a song he had penned for the presidential nominee, 'Harding, You're the Man for Us', which called Harding 'a man who'll make the White House / shine out just like a lighthouse', the Ohio Republican and owner of *The Marion Star* newspaper was guaranteed his term in the White House. If Donald Trump wanted to make America great again, Warren Harding wanted to make America normal again. Some things never change, even in one hundred years; and perhaps history really does repeat itself.

Whether we are aware of it or not, music is one of the most crucial foundations of life. It exists at our deepest level – that place inside us that reminds us of who we are and where we have come from. It is crucial to our formative years, in how we relate to lyrics of songs, and how they reflect the state of our lives at that time. It's why we associate particular songs with specific episodes and periods in our past. We play songs at weddings, funerals, anniversaries, and even during protests. Nursery rhymes colour the innocent worlds of our young children. Political rallies and presidential campaigns are often remembered years later for the songs they chose to spread their message.

Songwriters often tell me their music is a pure reflection of a life that often can't be lived in or adequately described by simply using bare words. The words become illuminated and permanently etched in our minds once the music is added and the song takes on a life of its own. Fighting on the battlefields of the First World War stopped on Christmas Eve in 1914 when a lone soldier's beautiful voice made history. 'Silent Night' became the Christmas song that stopped the war, if only for a day. It became known as the Christmas Truce. A single song briefly stopped a bloody war because it became a transpersonal power and united hearts. Music is a natural healer, giving back harmony and balance to an anxious mind or a troubled heart. It made perfect sense to me as a young man that music should be at the heart of everything I would do in my life. It still is today.

John Miles had a huge chart hit in 1976 with a song called 'Music'. Its opening line, where he describes music as his first love, in many ways sums up how I feel about the music that brought me to where I am today. If radio was at the core of my journey, then music was the vehicle I travelled on.

With the occasional break away from the microphone to try my hand at other projects, most of the last forty years have been spent in radio studios and I have loved dearly every single minute of the experience. I never went to college to train in media or journalism, or to learn how to become a radio presenter. I started out as a pirate at the age of eighteen, an illegal broadcasting activist who along with other young renegades and mavericks, and the occasional hippy-type, defiantly broke the silly Irish laws that prevented independent radio stations from choosing a vacant frequency and playing music to listeners.

Long before that, while other boys I went to school with were out kicking a football around our cul-de-sac late into the evening, I was sitting beside our vintage Pye Cambridge radio in the corner of our dining room every evening, tuning in to any remote frequency that played any type of music. Later on a clear night when the reception was good, I would gently tweak the circular knob on the radio and inch my way patiently along the longwave dial, tuning in to stations in places such as Moscow, or Vienna, or Hamburg, which had programmes consisting of mostly classical music. Their announcers spoke so fast and for so long in their native languages, I was always fascinated by how they never seemed to stop to catch their breath.

From my youngest years, there are the vaguest memories somewhere in my head of what I can only describe as musical moments that I just can't place; although, most often, people don't recall any memories from their earliest years of life, usually before age three or four, as a result of a type of 'baby-brain' fog psychologists call 'infantile amnesia'. I can remember my mother putting me down into my cot on some occasions and staring up at her in the soft light, but I have no recollection of the before or after of those split moments. I can remember her holding me steady in a shallow warm bath while I kicked and splashed the water onto the bathroom floor, but no recollections of anything else on those occasions.

When I was born in 1961, 'trad' (based on old-time New Orleans style traditional jazz) was the big craze on this side of the world, with Acker Bilk, Kenny Ball and Chris Barber at the forefront of the trend. A doo-wop revival was taking the States by storm, resulting in chart hits for groups like The Capris, Rosie and the Originals, and The Marcels.

On the day I started school in 1965, I was four and a half years old. The Rolling Stones were at the top of our music charts with '(I Can't Get No) Satisfaction', while The Beatles were number one in the States with 'Help' – two very appropriate song titles whenever I think back to my schooldays! Overall I never liked school, mostly because it got in the way of my daydreaming. I made a big impression that first morning by refusing to go inside to my classroom. I let it be known in quite a loud voice that I had changed my mind and that I was going home with my mother. To prove my point, I scaled the school's high perimeter railings and clung on as tightly as I could, refusing to come down unless the three teachers watching me agreed that I could go home.

All of the other students were by this time inside the small school building, except for another boy my own age who was watching my protest from below. Before I knew it, he had climbed up alongside me. The two of us waited, watching each other, clinging on desperately and not sure what would happen next. Eventually, after some forceful persuasion, we both lost our grips and fell off the fence. Because we were last into class, we ended up sitting beside each other in the one remaining empty desk, which was less than two feet from the teacher's table. The boy's name was Robbie, and we would remain best friends for many years.

During our first few weeks of that first term, Robbie discovered a small gap in the high wall towards the back of the schoolyard. Beyond it was a huge rambling cornfield known as Jack's Field, apparently owned by a farmer called Jack who had a notorious reputation, a huge dog, and a dislike for anyone who used his land as a shortcut to one of the local housing estates. Older boys would tell us how some of their friends had been caught by this Jack character and locked up in his barn without food or water for days. Whenever Robbie and I sat on top of the high yellow wall in the late afternoons, once the yard had emptied and the teachers had gone home for the day, we could just about make out the sloping roof of the huge corrugated red barn in question, at the bottom of the long field. No one knew if any of the stories were true. To the best of my memory, there never was a farmer called Jack, even though there was one boy in first class who captured the imaginations of the school beginners with stories of how he had been captured a week after he had started school and taken to the barn where he was tied up and held captive for an entire weekend.

I had a lot in common with Robbie. I was a boy of few words, a loner; so was Robbie. Neither of us was interested in the 'herd instinct' that was the unspoken rule of the schoolyard. We quickly learned that within every class there was a hierarchy of power, which usually manifested itself in the random scraps and fist fights that took place after school. The upper echelons of the hierarchy were usually made up of kids who would do anything to start a fight. The toughest scrapper was usually at the top; the quieter kids like us preferred to stay well clear of the gladiatorial warfare by finding a haystack to hide behind in Jack's field.

Robbie and I enjoyed the solitude together, often spending our lunchbreaks cowering behind the high yellow wall in the suntrap in a corner of Jack's field, enjoying peanut butter sandwiches and mini-bottles of creamy full-fat milk. I have little recollection what we spent our time talking about during those days: maybe television, as we were both fans of *The Time Tunnel*, a science-fiction series about two young scientists who invented a time tunnel and then accidentally became trapped in their own invention. James Weldon Johnson, African-American activist and lawyer, said in his 1912 novel *The Autobiography of an Ex-Colored Man*: 'The people in your childhood are the ones that you will miss the most when you are an adult.' Weldon Johnson was right. When I look back, I realise Robbie and I shared so much of what it means to navigate the childhood and teenage years and to start to make sense of a life that guarantees you nothing. In the beginning you are not expected to do very much, other than simply turn up. But somewhere out along the road, we cross an invisible line where we realise that life has become a game of survival. We are not competing against anyone except ourselves, and that is the cruellest contest imaginable. As we grow, we become more conscious of the personality traits and the qualities inbuilt in us that we don't like. We find something about us that we come to believe makes us unappealing to others, and before we know it these 'silent shortcomings' become the filtered lenses through which we look at the world around us, and how we think that world looks at us.

I wore black-rimmed glasses when I was eight, and I became known as Piggy. Looking back, I can only presume the nickname came from the boy in William Golding's *Lord of the Flies*, in which a plane evacuating a group of schoolboys from Britain is shot down over a deserted tropical island. Piggy was always seen as the most rational and intelligent among the group of stranded boys because of his wire-rimmed spectacles, and his glasses represented the studious type – trying your hardest to succeed and achieve. It was years later, while reading the book as a teenager in secondary school, that I realised the story's underlying theme – that no matter what we would like to believe, the thin line between civil order and inherent evil is prone to blurring given the right circumstances. And so, because I did my homework neatly and was attentive in class, I became known as 'Piggy' the day I arrived into school with my new glasses.

Robbie and I remained best friends for many years until he moved to a brand-new school that had opened closer to where he lived. The world of a young boy was a very small and limited place back then, so our paths parted at the beginning of the summer holidays some years later. I recall he went to County Clare with his family for the duration of the summer, and when the September day arrived when we were due to start our new term in school, Robbie wasn't there. Our friendship petered out as life took Robbie in a different direction. It would take another thirty-two years for us to meet again and sit down together, in more difficult circumstances, where our lives bore no resemblance to those carefree days we had spent gazing out across a golden cornfield. Days when, surrounded by beech, larch and chestnut trees in the sunshine, we would look for fallen chestnuts still sealed in their spikey green hulls, and enjoy the simple boyhood pleasure of playing conkers.

I'm about to turn sixty as I write this, and as I look back over the years I can see early warnings of my later experiences with depression in my early forties – way back in the distant times when I was that small boy in Jack's field. I can sense that boy's vulnerability (even though he would never have heard the word before, nor have had a clue what it meant). But I know back then I was vulnerable: 'prone to bouts of depression', some would say.

It's only in recent years that research has shown that the roots of depression are planted at the earliest age, shortly after a small child becomes aware of their surroundings, their own consciousness, and their conscience. What Robbie could never have known was that in later years I would become depressed to the point where I questioned the meaning and purpose of my life, and whether or not it was even worth struggling on with. And what I couldn't have known was that Robbie would find himself in exactly the same place, at exactly the same time as I did. I sometimes wonder if that was why we became instant friends that morning on our first day in school. Could there have been some sort of synchronicity that brought us together, as each of us somehow unconsciously recognised similar traits in the other that we could both identify with? I genuinely believe that this was the case.

I would dearly love to spend even one hour with Robbie now, an hour where we are five years old or ten years old again; I'd love us to be able to share our experiences, good and bad, and to relate to each other all we have learned since then.

When it came to a career, I veered away from the obvious choices my friends were opting for. I needed a purpose, or some sort of objective that would give real meaning to my life. I had this innate feeling from a very early age that music just had to be a part of my life, whatever direction that would take. I didn't want a job that didn't include music. Music was like an escape hatch for me from those strange bouts of sadness that I often felt as a young child. There was never really a specific reason why I felt sad as a boy as young as eight or nine; but one thing I knew for certain was that music made me feel better, stronger. Maybe the sadness would always be there in some shape or form, but music lifted me above it. Music was like a magic door. My life needed music. Eventually I would realise that my career needed it too.

The summer of 1976 still stands out in my mind as one of the most amazing and exhilarating periods in my life, and was the reason why radio was always my real calling. I had discovered that new-found freedom that comes with the mid-teen years. I was an adult (or at least I thought I was). I had just finished my Intermediate Certificate exams (Junior Certificate as it's known today) and the warmest summer in living memory had just started. It was a heatwave the like of which I had never known.

The feeling of waking up on those bright, warm mornings with sunshine streaming through the curtains into my bedroom was exhilarating. Those days were like a rite of passage, an in-between time as if I had been able to step off the treadmill of the school timetable mentality and the discipline of uniforms, schoolbags, textbooks, essays and exams; my diary was wiped clean. I was a free agent. Flared jeans and striped t-shirts were all we wore. There was no pressure on me to do anything other than enjoy what felt like endless sunny days with their high, blue skies and scorching, record-breaking temperatures.

Music became my compass in 1976. It was everywhere, and the chart songs from that year are still among the greatest radio classics of all time. Elton John and Kiki Dee's 'Don't Go Breaking My Heart', ABBA's 'Dancing Queen', John Miles' 'Music', and Thin Lizzy's 'The Boys Are Back In Town' became the soundtrack of the hottest summer on record. And then there was Motown, with Diana Ross and Stevie Wonder; the Sound of Philadelphia, with Harold Melvin &

the Blue Notes, and the O'Jays; Warner, Elektra, Asylum ... I was beginning to read the catalogues and the background stories of artists who belonged to different record labels.

So many exciting things were happening around me that summer when I was fifteen. The heat of the sunshine and the melody of the music made me wish every day that this time in my life would never end. It was hard to keep up. And music radio at last was beginning to grow and find its feet among a hungry audience. Radio Luxembourg – the Great 208 – was still the number-one choice when it came to radio listening. Nighttime was Radio Luxembourg's territory. The signal on the medium wave band improved with the night atmosphere and I would will myself to stay awake into the early hours, listening to the DJs who laid the foundation of my love for radio. Stuart Henry, Peter Powell, Paul Burnett, and my favourite, Benny Brown became heroes in our house, even though they were broadcasting from a tiny city a thousand miles away. Their pace of delivery and their friendly style was infectious; and they always sounded like they were having the best time ever.

RTÉ was slowly beginning to get its act together when it came to playing the chart music everyone wanted to hear. During that hot summer, Radio Éireann split its medium wave and VHF frequencies, so that the more mundane radio shows could be listened to on medium wave, while every afternoon on VHF (which would later become known as FM), Larry Gogan played the hit songs that would become the indelible soundtrack for so many of us from that generation. It was the best music around. It was a mixture of international and local talent, as the Irish showband scene was thriving in the mid-seventies.

I might have been barely fifteen, but that didn't stop me from wanting to have my own radio show. I remember one afternoon when I had the house to myself, I decided to make a phone call. Like many households back then, we had a landline phone sitting on our neat little hall table. It was an ivory-coloured GPO 746 rotary phone on which you dialled each of your numbers slowly in a clockwise direction while you held the receiver to your ear. I had decided that I was going to call RTÉ.

I asked the woman who answered so pleasantly if

I could talk to someone about becoming a DJ. She told me to hold while she transferred my call. Within seconds I was chatting to a man whose voice I instantly recognised. It was Larry Gogan. I couldn't believe that someone as famous as Larry was taking unsolicited calls like this. I explained to him that I wanted more than anything else to be a DJ on the radio.

Larry explained to me that an education was important, and good results in my exams would stand to me. 'And of course you have to know lots about the different singers who you will be playing on your show.'

I reassured him I already did. I got the feeling he was expecting me to ask if there were any vacancies going in RTÉ that week.

'How old are you?' he asked.

I coughed. 'Nearly sixteen,' I replied, trying to deepen my voice.

'Well, study hard, listen to all sorts of music, and learn as much as you can about the singers and the bands. And always appreciate the hard work that goes into writing and recording a great song. Save up your money and buy some of the music magazines, like

Spotlight. They're very good for helping you to keep up to date with all that's happening.'

I thanked him for his time. It was only after I ended the call that I realised that Larry had spent almost forty minutes talking to me. That was it. The decision had been made for me. I convinced myself that if I'd had a voice that wasn't suitable for the job, Larry wouldn't have spent so long on the call. It's amazing what you can convince yourself of if you really want to believe it's true! That call set me on a path to what would become a forty-year career doing a job I loved. The biggest surprise for me was that Larry remembered that phone call, all of thirteen years later when I finally was given the opportunity to join RTÉ 2FM. Just before I started my first show on weekday afternoons on the station, Larry walked into my studio and shook my hand with the words, 'It might have taken you fourteen years, but you finally got here. Well done.' Radio presenting has been in my blood, programmed into my DNA, for as far back as I can remember and it seemed like the best job in the world even if I took a few detours on the way.

I led a varied life after leaving school. My first job,

at the age of seventeen, was in Switzers, a famous upmarket department store in Grafton Street in Dublin where Brown Thomas is these days. I was assigned to the bedding department on the second floor where I learned the art of selling bed linen, pillowcases, and the much-talked-about duvet, which was trending as the very latest 'must have' bedroom fashion accessory in those days. People who shopped in Switzers never appeared to be short of money, and they tipped well. While the customers were pleasant, the work was boring. I remember coming in before six o'clock one morning to prepare the bed display in one of the shop's front windows ahead of the post-Christmas sales which started later that morning. I had been out very late the night before with some friends, so I decided to lie down on the bed for an hour before the morning got bright and the store opened. I thought the laughter I could hear was part of a dream I'd been having until I opened my eyes and realised a large crowd had gathered on the street outside the window, watching me sprawled across the bed fast asleep. Later that day, after a good telling off, the personnel manager thought I would be better suited to working in the music department, down in Switzers' basement.

The job was bliss, considering how much I loved music. I spent the days selling vinyl records and cassettes, playing all of my own favourite songs on the hi-fi system beneath the counter, while taking charge in the afternoons of the security entrance used by the shop's workers, where they would clock in using their time cards first thing every morning, and then clock back out when they were leaving in the evening. At least that's what was meant to happen. A good few lads enjoyed popping out at lunchtime every day for a few pints in the International Bar nearby in Exchequer Street. It wasn't uncommon for some of them not to bother coming back to work. On those occasions, with a familiar wink and a nod, I was under strict unspoken instructions to punch their cards for them discreetly at the time they would normally be expected to go home. I was tipped handsomely at the end of most weeks and no one knew any different for as long as I worked there, which in fairness wasn't that long.

In early 1979 I became serious about careers

– or so I thought – and took a job with Irish Life Assurance Company, in Abbey Street in Dublin, where I would work in the Group Pensions section by day and study for the ACCA accountancy exams every evening. The intention of the company was to train me up as a certified accountant. I quickly realised I had different intentions, however. Pirate radio stations were popping up all around the country, and I couldn't resist the offer of my own radio show. It still amazes me how an eighteen-year-old could survive on three and a half hours' sleep a night: I had a full time nine-to-five job in Irish Life, but before that I presented a breakfast show on a pirate station called ARD, then went home to study for accountancy exams each evening before going out with a case full of records to gig in a city-centre nightclub until 2 a.m. the next morning. Then home to bed an hour later and up at 6.30 a.m. to start it all again. Eventually a choice had to be made: a secure future in accountancy and life assurance, or a radio show on a pirate station where you never knew from one day to the next whether you were going to have a job to go to. It would eventually be radio;

but before pursuing that fulltime, I decided to do something that didn't come as much of a surprise to most people who knew me. I decided to study for the priesthood.

I was brought up in the traditions of the Catholic Church – like almost everyone I knew back in 1970s Ireland. I sang in the church choir as a young boy and I became an altar server. I was twenty when I made this decision to become a priest, a regular churchgoer, and closely connected to many of the activities associated with my local church, including being an active member of the parish folk group, and helping out as sacristan during many of the ceremonial occasions that were central to our local community, including the visit in 1979 of the then pope, John Paul II.

To this day I can understand why I would have wanted to become a priest back then. I was drawn to the ministry by its basic purpose of reaching out to others, and its reliance on a strong faith which sustained those who committed in every way to live by it. Of course it was never as simple or as straightforward as that. I have never been motivated by materialism or wealth. Reaching out to others has always been something that felt natural to me. So after many months of consideration, I decided it was a path I would follow in the hope that I was making the right choice.

A few days before making my decision public, I visited an elderly nun at the enclosed Carmelite convent in Dublin. Members of enclosed religious orders separate themselves from the affairs of the outside world, and accept that once they join the order they will never leave the confines of their convent. I had been told that she was a deeply spiritual person who would help to dispel any doubts I might have.

Despite what some may say, I don't believe that the cloistered life is a selfish ministry, or a self-centred form of lifelong meditation. Such orders, even to this day, believe that their prayers will touch the lives of people all over the world who are suffering or in need of the prayers of others. The afternoon I visited Sister Rachel, I was taken to a small room and invited to sit in a very basic wooden armchair. I was facing a small wire-framed grille, which sat in front of a purple curtain. I could hear the hollow sound of a door closing somewhere. The light was dim in the room beyond the curtain and I could just about make out the shape of a woman's face surrounded by a black veil and what looked like a medieval starched white wimple. I could see her smile and bow her head. She invited me to listen to a special prayer she then recited which included my name. Suddenly I was almost overcome with a feeling of joy. It felt as though I was exactly where I was meant to be at that precise moment. It was an experience I will never forget. It's always with me, even all these years later.

I expected our conversation to last ten, maybe fifteen minutes, but two hours later as twilight made the two separated rooms even darker, we were still talking to each other. It was one of the most uplifting days of my life. I told her I had been abused as a young boy by a member of a religious order and that I was finding it so difficult to accept the doctrine of priesthood, if the same church that I imagined serving for the remainder of my life was going to continue to allow paedophiles to hide behind their priestly collars while destroying the lives of innocent children. She told me that I was never to allow that to stand in the way of my freedom to choose what was most important for me in the years ahead. 'Abusers are drawn to this life because those who are lost in the world, who come to us for support and guidance, are vulnerable, and they make easy prey for those whose hearts and minds are instructed and guided by evil, not by a kind and loving God. There are abusers in every walk of life, not just in the spiritual life.' I will remember her words forever.

For the year or so I studied in college, Sister Rachel became my spiritual adviser. I visited her once a fortnight, on a Wednesday afternoon for two hours, and thoroughly enjoyed our chats. Despite her detachment from the life I was more familiar with, she knew more about life than most people I have ever met. Because I was a seminary student, allowances were made for the curtain to be drawn back during my visits so that we could see each other clearly. She was beautiful, and for a woman in her seventies, wore the face of someone much younger.

Looking back, I realise just how important her role was in a 'calling' I had briefly chosen to follow. The place of an enclosed nun who has devoted her life to prayer, silence and detachment might seem outdated, even bizarre, in today's society, but when we look beyond the restrictive and limiting beliefs of traditional religions, we are really challenged by an opportunity to understand the true calling and purpose in this life of people like Sister Rachel. The only word I can find to describe Sister Rachel's place in my life, albeit for a short time, is transpersonal, which means areas of consciousness beyond the limits of personal identity, or those areas of the mind which search for higher meanings in life. Sister Rachel's belonging existed beyond the earthly world we are all so familiar with. I've often found myself saying, 'there's got to be more to life than this'; Sister Rachel was my guide in finding higher meanings in my life.

I've often heard it said that people who devote themselves to a life of singular spirituality have little worthwhile experience to offer in the day-to-day lives of those who choose to marry and raise children. I've also sadly heard people refer to them as selfish. I don't agree. This gentle, caring nun was capable of seeing far beyond much of what goes on in the busy lives of relationships and marriage, the tireless task of raising children and trying to create a work/life balance. Because she wasn't burdened by the exhaustive commitments of a life outside the cloistered walls of an enclosed order, Sister Rachel was in a perfect position to address the more pressing demands and needs of the soul – that part of each of us that rarely gets the attention and care it needs. The soul isn't concerned about anything except its relationship with the real purpose, and those higher meanings that exist within our true selves, that each of us must find in order to make sense of this one life that we experience within a limited time and space.

Eventually I would have to break the news to her that I was leaving my studies and would not be devoting my life to the priesthood. I couldn't get my head around the vow of celibacy – the benefits of remaining single and un-attached for the rest of my life. Why shouldn't a good man (or woman) be allowed to marry, yet still carry out the word of God in the true role of the priestly ministry? The Protestant religion doesn't have a problem with it. I wanted to be a father. I wanted intimacy. I wanted a companion. In addition, I couldn't see the sense in locking oneself away for seven years in a college behind huge walls. Surely a priest can only become educated in his ministry if he is among his people from his earliest training – aware of their needs, and equipped with life's teachings to know how to support them. Sister Rachel remained calm as I explained why I had decided to leave, that I really believed I wasn't cut out to be an ordained priest. I also hinted that I really wanted to go back to radio, and then she smiled. 'You don't need to be a priest to do the work that lies ahead of you. Each of us is born to minister to the needs of someone. It is the reason why each of us is here.' I felt humbled. I also felt an awkward distance between us for the first time since meeting her. I knew we most likely would never meet again, and for me that was the saddest part of my departure. Her final words to me were, 'You will have many meetings like this in your life, so you will never feel alone once you find your true purpose.' Sister Rachel is long gone, as is her sense of serenity and acceptance, but I can still recall how she urged me to be forever mindful of the importance of serenity in the midst of uncertainty – something that's not always as easy as it sounds.

So here I was thirty-six years later, February 2018, in the midst of a storm of heartbreaking uncertainty. Life felt like it had been reduced to a tiny space of solitary confinement. It's not easy to find serenity in the uncertainty I was suddenly faced with after first hearing my own news, and then knowing that my parents had an agonising wait to hear my father's news.

After visiting my parents that day, uncertain and worried about what lay ahead, I stood on the platform at Broombridge railway station, waiting for the 13.11 train that would take me into Connolly, followed by a fifteen-minute walk to work. Unlike life, my daily train ran like clockwork. Out north beyond Dublin city I stared up into the clear blue sky and watched Flight EI147 as I did most days, give or take ten minutes to allow for departure. Aer Lingus's A330 climbed gracefully in its ascent at the start of its eleven-hour journey to San Francisco.

Most days its gliding serenity would take my breath away. That day, though, I was lost in a grief I had never known before.

For a brief moment it was 1986 again; and I was travelling to the USA on a Boeing 747, for the first time in my life. I was twenty-five then, and I felt young, alive and energised – as if my life was about to explode with new opportunities. I remember looking down that morning as the huge jet banked right and climbed, and how I was able to identify my parents' house which I had left three hours earlier. Now I gazed up at a transatlantic plane that most likely was also transporting another twenty-five-year-old beyond his old familiar world for the very first time.

My train approached the platform. My world couldn't have seemed any smaller or more frightening than it did at that moment. I felt exhausted. It was more of a deep, dull, cellular fatigue, stranger than anything I had ever experienced before. My body was home now to these strange sensations and tremors that I had no control over; I felt like I was withering inside.

I was terrified of what lay ahead of me – and now something inside was telling me I was about to lose my wonderful father. My eyes filled up and tears streamed down my face as I watched the plane through the train window as it moved further away into the western sky, climbing higher and higher and eventually disappearing from view.

Despite all that had happened in those few short hours that morning, I was now on my way into a radio studio where I would present my daily afternoon show – a mixture of music and chat – as if nothing out of the ordinary had happened and it was just a typical day. It was the same thing every day, though I now felt a fear I had never experienced before; and deep down my heart was breaking for whatever it was that was lurking just around the corner.

I often wonder what my dad must have been thinking that day as I said goodbye and pulled the door closed behind me. I'm just so glad I told him that I loved him, before I left them both to go to work. I can't remember the last time I had said those words to him – words that too often remain stifled and stunted within a silent, nervous reluctance until we realise it's too late to give them their voice. It just felt so important that day that I did. 'I love you too,' he had replied.

The doctor called my mother later that afternoon to say that the results of my father's blood tests were back. He asked her if they could both call to the surgery to see him for a chat the following morning. The results showed definite traces of cancer in a number of locations.

He died eight weeks later.

We buried my father on a soft April spring morning. There is a crippling sense of finality, so abrupt, when words utterly fail you, as you watch the coffin of someone you love being lowered into a deep hole in the ground. All they have ever stood for, all they have achieved in life – their accomplishments and their regrets, their joy and their suffering – are recalled in an instant at the graveside. Those joyful moments on happier spring mornings spent sitting at a kitchen table putting the world to rights all seemed like long ago; we would never again have a conversation, never share a joke or sit in silence as we savoured the unique taste of my mother's toast.

My father committed his long life to hard work. It was only in his final ten years that we both really came to know each other, and for that time I will be eternally grateful. Prior to that, I travelled a lot with my own work. Whenever I got to spend time at home, my daughters were always my priority. Similarly, my dad, Joe, spent most of our younger years travelling all over the world, building up a business he remained proud of for the rest of his life.

During Dad's final weeks I was undergoing a battery of medical tests. I visited him in hospital as often as I could. Nearing the end of his days he had become so ill that all we could do was sit with him and chat. With closed eyes he would occasionally nod and smile, perhaps to let us know that he was listening.

The night he died, Paula and I had left him to go home for a few hours' rest. The doctor had told me that it wouldn't be long, that it was likely he would pass away in the next few hours. Earlier that day the palliative care consultant, a gentle, empathic man with a soft voice, explained to me that Dad would be staying in the care of the hospital staff. They had hoped to move him to hospice care, but he had become so ill in the space of a couple of hours that the time remaining would be very brief.

My mother, Eileen and my sister, Amy stayed with him while we raced back home in the hope of resting for an hour or two. Neither of us bothered to undress or get into the bed. We simply lay on the duvet and held hands.

Looking back on that night, I realise now that in such heartbreaking moments we can find ourselves living an almost split-level existence for a short time. On one level, someone we dearly love is slipping away into death, and we allow ourselves to acknowledge the emotions and dwell on the memories that accompany the end of the long journey of a life well lived. Meanwhile, on another level, life around us still goes on as if nothing out of the ordinary is happening. It's as though we are snatched out of our comfort zones as our day-to-day lives are put on hold by the despair of what we know is now imminent, as we spend some time in that unfamiliar transpersonal place waiting for the confirmation of sad news.

The phone rang at 3.25 a.m., shaking us out of a light sleep. It was my brother, calling from home. His calming voice told me we had possibly less than an hour to get back to the hospital. Paula and I arrived just as my dad was taking his final breaths. He died peacefully that morning at 4.40 a.m., the cheek of his face resting gently against the palm of my mother's hand.

Chapter 5

LOSS, DEPRESSION AND THERAPY

Something inside me weakened following my father's death. My familiar life felt off-balance, as though it had become unhinged. In the days and weeks after his funeral, all I wanted was to run into my favourite park, close to where I lived then, and hide among the trees, trees that felt like they had been there forever. I might find peace there. I felt like a small dog that had fallen hard from a great height. I remained outwardly strong, until no one could see me. Funeral arrangements carry certain expectations. For some, there is an emotional protocol attached where no one should see your resolve weakening. After the short burial ceremony, Paula and I chose to spend the remainder of the day alone together.

Looking back, I knew that my father's days among us were coming to an end. I remember very little specifically about those weeks, apart from the medical tests and scans and examinations that seemed to fill my diary as my neurologist tried to diagnose what was wrong with me. All that time my dad was never far from my thoughts. Maybe that's why the seriousness of my illness never really struck home. I was always looking for opportunities in between work and my own appointments to call in to see him and spend some time together. Maybe that was the reason why my own diagnosis hit me so hard, coming so soon after his death. He was no longer there to visit. He was gone, leaving in his wake an awful emptiness. Whenever I experienced his physical absence I reminded myself that he was walking beside me through all this, supporting me in a way that gave me huge comfort and reassurance. It was as though he was now in a place, beyond the limitations of time and space, where he could instil in me occasional hints of clarity that I found impossible to find anywhere else. Whereas I couldn't see beyond my own horizon, it felt as though he could. It felt like he was looking out for me from a place that I couldn't comprehend in my mind, but a place that my heart seemed drawn to. This gave me a strength I needed so badly.

It was as if the ground was constantly shifting beneath my feet, and it brought me back to the late nineties when I had last found myself in the grip of severe depression. Back then, my life was changing, and much of the change felt out of my control, as I was trying secretly to deal with a darkness inside me that was slowly destroying me – apart from one bright moment when my youngest daughter Aibhín was born on 7 November 1997. It was one of the happiest days of my life. I will never forget how blessed I felt to hold her moments after she entered this world, and to watch her grow tall and strong in the years that followed. There were two other equally happy days before then of course, when my older daughters, Kerri and Katie, were born, but when I look back, I genuinely believe that Aibhín's arrival saved me. New life is perhaps one of the greatest antidotes to the darkness of depression. Seeing my tiny baby begin her journey in this life was a poignant reminder that I was also once like this. From the moment we become aware of our surroundings as small babies, fear becomes our greatest emotion, even though we don't understand what fear is. The only reassurance a helpless baby wants is the presence and attention of its mother, or father. Then it feels safe. Aibhín's arrival made me realise that this tiny child needed her father also, in the same way her older sisters did. If I were to take my own life, then I wouldn't be there to protect them ever again from the fear that we all feel for a multitude of reasons throughout our lives. My own fear at that time was that if I was dead by suicide, then they might go through the rest of their lives believing that I didn't care about them, that I didn't love them enough to stay alive and look after them. Her sisters were nine and seven. They also needed me, but this tiny new life was only just beginning. I wanted them to know always that I loved them, and they would always come first.

I felt hopeful that night for the first time in so long, but that hope would be brief. I realised that this life of mine was bound up in commitments to a baby who needed me – not only because her tiny life was my responsibility, but because I loved her. The only way she would overcome her helplessness as a newborn baby was to grow and learn about her own life. Her arrival made me realise that the only way I would overcome my own helplessness at that time was to find a purpose that would give meaning to my life. Little did she realise at that stage that her arrival would help me find a purpose.

Almost a year after Aibhín was born I took over RTÉ 2FM's flagship breakfast show, which aired from 7 a.m. until 9 a.m. each morning. The previous presenter, Ian Dempsey, had left the station to take over Today FM's breakfast show; so I was now in direct competition with Ireland's favourite early-morning DJ. Ian had been presenting breakfast on

2FM for nineteen years, so there was an overall expectation that his loyal fans would simply move the dial to continue listening to the man whose voice was usually the first one they heard when their alarm clocks went off every morning. As it turned out, the audience remained divided for the two years I presented 2FM breakfast. He might have taken half of the daily listenership, but the other half decided they were comfortable enough to stay with me.

At the time, the depression felt like a non-stop struggle for survival. I found myself having to drag my way through my radio show each morning as best I could, minute by minute, driving every ounce of energy I could muster into sounding positive. I kept reminding myself that I was free once the nine o'clock news jingle was played. Then I could climb into my car and go home to bed; or, as I would often do, drive to a remote part of the Phoenix Park, turn off the engine and fall asleep for hours. There were some mornings when it almost became too hard to pretend any longer. They were the mornings I had to remind myself that I had three beautiful daughters, one who was barely one year old. I wanted her to know me as she was growing up, not remembering a father by his photograph; a father who took his own life when all she wanted was to grow up beside him knowing he would be there for her. Her big sisters needed a father to come home from school to. The sense of despair was slowly tearing me apart. I felt as though I had no control over this depression. On those days I distracted my warped, negative thinking by concentrating on a plan I had been slowly hatching somewhere in my head about walking out of the radio station mid-show and never coming back.

I had this perfectly rational scheme whereby I would leave the studio during the news break, walk briskly to the car park as though I was collecting something from my car, and then drive the hundred miles or so to Rosslare, where I would board the afternoon ferry for Le Havre, in France. Once there I could drive anywhere. I loved France, everything about it: its seasons, its wine, its food, its language, its indomitable spirit. I could arrive into one of its thirty-two thousand remote villages. I could change my identity and start a new life in Castlenou, neatly secluded deep in the Pyrenees, or Mittelbergheim, famous for its wine; or maybe Collioure, close to the Spanish border with its Catalan culture. I would never be found for as long as I wanted to remain in absentia. I could leave behind everything that was slowly killing me and start all over again. I was plagued by this feeling, that if I didn't run away and reinvent myself I was going to die. By removing myself from the root of the problem, I could stay alive. Of course, the root of the problem lay within me.

In reality I knew that this disappearing act was completely mad: all I would be doing was taking my depression with me. It would stare at me from the passenger seat throughout my journey, mocking me. I would also be deserting my children, and for that alone I knew I could never forgive myself. I loved them too much to do such a mindless thing. Anyway, I figured I would end up somehow having my picture taken, sitting outside some small café, by a couple of Irish backpackers cycling by tandem across Europe. Or, worse, being 'outed' by a French tabloid with the headline 'DJ Irlandais manquant retrouvé vivant' – 'Missing Irish DJ found alive'. And for evermore

I would be known as the Irish DJ who had lost his mind.

I'm always hearing that attitudes to mental health problems are changing. They're not, from what I can see. Maybe there's a lot more depression today, or perhaps more people who hid their depression for years, much like me, are too exhausted to keep it a secret anymore. It's hard work pretending that you're not depressed; and of course pretending you're not depressed will not make your depression go away.

While much has been done to explain depression, and why some people get depressed, there is still very little empathy or support for those who suffer to the point where they become suicidal. It shouldn't have to be like that.

If we can learn anything from the lockdown restrictions imposed by the COVID-19 pandemic, these awful days of solitary confinement will hopefully prove how much damage a disrupted routine can do to the already fragile mind of someone who suffers from anxiety and depression. Every day I listen to the statistics of the number of people who have tested positive for coronavirus, along with the numbers of those who have died. I have yet to hear anyone say that some of these deaths were the result of suicide – the end result of neglecting those who are emotionally unable to cope with the isolation, fear, lack of belonging and connection to whatever gave them hope and purpose before these enforced lockdowns cut off their social oxygen supply.

One of the many problems caused by depression is the inability to focus on something that allows you to have a continuum of thought. Without a regular routine, the human mind enters a state of chaos, in which there is no logical reason to anything. This eventually leads to hopelessness because the person no longer has that safety connection – a sense of belonging. Perhaps I am fortunate in that writing has helped me in dark times to maintain some form of focus and a sense of belonging. Even during this difficult period in my own life many years ago, I was able to write my second novel, *The Keeper*, and to see it through until its publication in 1999. But when I thumb back through its pages, as I did recently, I can still feel the darkness that permeated my life back then.

What might seem rational and normal to someone who is severely depressed might appear to be the complete opposite to those who are witnessing this deterioration up close. As I sank deeper into a depressed state, I wasn't really consciously aware of anything unusual, except those feelings of overwhelming apathy that would visit me in giant waves, sometimes lasting a few hours, while other times flooring me for days. I started to write *A Day Called Hope*, once I began to emerge from this dark period and was able to see that experiencing strong negative emotions randomly now and then is not necessarily a sign of depression, but that when you find yourself subject to lots of different emotions at the one time and for an extended period – such as sadness, anger, self-loathing, futility, hopelessness and apathy – then you need support.

By the time *The Keeper* was published in 1999, I had started on a course of antidepressants and stopped drinking alcohol for a number of years. I like to believe that the medication restored me to some semblance of functional normality, but I can't honestly say that feeling better was due entirely to the medication because neither scientists nor psychiatrists fully understand the role that antidepressants play in lifting depression.

Maybe antidepressants should be likened to a form of anaesthetic. While they can sometimes temporarily relieve emotional pain, nothing is going to completely alleviate depression until you remove from your life whatever is causing you to feel depressed. If you can't get to the root of what's causing your depression and address it, then no amount of antidepressant medication will ever fully lift that lingering sense of hopelessness.

In the 1990s psychotherapy was almost unheard of here in Ireland; it was certainly only a fledgling therapy. Yet in the USA, every A-list actor seemed to have their own therapist. It would take me another couple of years to face up to my own demons, after finally throwing in the towel and admitting to myself that I needed help.

In 2001, in an effort to make sense of and rebuild my crumbling inner world, I made an appointment to see a psychologist. A friend of mine had recommended her – a kind woman in her early sixties, who sat and listened to me for almost an hour as I tried to explain what was wrong with me – even though I wasn't sure what exactly was wrong with me. I started by telling her what I did for a living. She asked me about my children, about life at home, and about the people I worked with. She asked me to tell her about aspects of my life that made me sad. This was my very first encounter with a therapist and I had no idea why she was asking these questions. We had just started to delve into my childhood and my teenage years when she announced that the session was over. It was at that point that I asked her directly if she thought there was actually anything wrong with me. She didn't give me a straight answer, simply suggesting that we meet for another few sessions to discuss different aspects of my life a little further. I left her office that afternoon, never to return.

Maybe I thought she could sort out my problem in one session, like a visit to the doctor often results in a prescription for antibiotics. I knew very little about psychotherapy back then. I felt that my visit had been worthwhile though as, instead of a prescription, she recommended a book called *Beyond Prozac* by an Irish doctor called Terry Lynch. It was as though Terry had written this just for me. Every page shouted its words straight at my face. I took it everywhere with me. I even found myself reading half a page here and there during my afternoon radio show, which I had been reinstated to in late 2000 after I asked to be relieved of breakfast show duties. My natural home was afternoon radio. Looking back, it was the time of the day when my voice and my enthusiasm were at their best. I was happiest when I was *Gareth O'Callaghan in the Afternoon*.

My visit to the psychologist that afternoon in 2001 inadvertently led me to get to know Terry Lynch, to whom I will be eternally grateful for helping me to realise that there was a way out of my darkness. Terry has devoted his entire working life to helping people deal with health problems, concentrating exclusively in recent years on mental health, in particular depression. He has done trojan work in educating his fellow GPs on how they can help their patients without always relying on psychotropic medication.

However, my visit that day also opened a dark door from my childhood, a door I thought I had closed years before, a horrific chapter I thought I had dealt with and moved beyond.

For most of my life, I have been fascinated by how the mind works, so it's hardly surprising that as I struggled with this period of depression I started to track down more books and other writings that could help me figure out what exactly was 'not right' with me. I was hungry for answers to the questions that would not go away. At the time, there was a huge ignorance around depression, many people saw it as a character weakness and an excuse to cop out of daily life. I was beginning to see it in a much different light. But I was starved of the information I needed – where would I find it?

I had always been interested in hypnosis, in how the conscious mind can be distracted to the point where a hypnotherapist can delve into the unconscious mind in an effort to bring about positive change in a person's life. The human brain is divided between the conscious mind and the unconscious mind. The conscious mind is what you are using right now to read these words; but later you will rely on your unconscious mind to recall what you have read. You might recall it tomorrow, or maybe not until next year; but the unconscious mind stores that information carefully for you, so that you can recall it in an instant if you need to.

The conscious mind is primarily tasked with the present moment. It's our main filter for how we view the world right now, whether we are driving, or talking, or thinking, or typing. The unconscious mind however deals with memory storage, emotional reactions, recalling all the information you learned over years when it comes to sitting an important exam. It helps you to drive your car, without your conscious mind having to recall every single manoeuvre it takes to drive from work to home. If you had to remind yourself every single time you sat into your car to press down on the clutch to put the car in first gear while indicating right as you gently put pressure on the accelerator, and not forgetting to release the hand break, while checking in your mirrors to see if it's safe for you to leave your parking position, you would go mad. So instead, the unconscious mind remembers all this important information for you, and feeds it to you instantaneously so that you can get on with checking that the children are safely buckled into their seat belts in the back seat and their doors are locked.

Hypnosis is about tapping into the depths of the unconscious mind: it distracts the conscious mind, placing it in a lazy altered state so that the therapist can gain access to the much deeper unconscious mind. Here, all the memories of the past are stored in such a way that they can be recalled and re-enacted in the present.

It all really started for me one Saturday morning in 2001, while I was browsing in a second-hand bookshop. I found a book called *Hypnotherapy*, written by Dave Elman. Elman was one of the most important hypnotists of the twentieth century. Born in 1900, he was a radio host, a songwriter and a jazz musician. He was inspired to research hypnosis when his father, who was dying from cancer, told him that he had received pain relief through hypnosis, which gave him the opportunity to play live on stage with his son one more time before he died. Elman's further research into hypnosis after his father's death helped him to discover ways of hypnotising his clients in just ten seconds. He became a huge star on the vaudeville circuit with his hypnosis show, but his real interest came years later when he realised the potential of the speed of the hypnotic induction, and its powerful use in medicine.

Around this time I also discovered the writings of one of the greatest masters of hypnotherapy, a genius called Milton H. Erickson. Born in 1901, Erickson was an American psychiatrist and psychologist, specialising in medical hypnosis and family therapy. As a young boy, books were so expensive and scarce that he decided to read the dictionary from start to finish, repeatedly, in an effort to become educated in the power of words in the English language and to overcome what he called his dyslexia. As a young man stricken with polio and left bed-bound and severely paralysed for many years, his interest in hypnosis grew as he explored its potential to promote self-healing. He slowly started to recall 'body memories' associated with the muscular movements of his own body. By concentrating on these memories, he was able to teach his muscles how to work again by gently focusing his mental energy on them, and tweaking them through hypnosis. As a result, his muscles slowly regained control of parts of his body, which eventually enabled him to talk and use his arms again. This would later contribute to the study of 'muscle memory', and how the nucleus of each muscle cell retains the memories of its past development and is capable of restoring itself, through deep hypnosis, to a level of renewed strength even after long periods of inaction. Much speculation still surrounds how exactly hypnosis contributed to his recovery; but I am always reminded that hypnosis remains a highly subjective and imprecise field that relies on so many different variables and conditions in order to determine its outcome.

Erickson believed, through his work, that the unconscious mind was so self-creative, it could generate its own solutions to problems that were causing anxiety and depression at a conscious level. Spurred on by my interest in Erickson's work, I enrolled in a number of evening and weekend courses in psychology and counselling that I had seen advertised in the national newspapers. I also travelled to England over many weekends (and some weeks) to take other courses in the subject. Eventually I gathered together the qualifications I needed in order to become a psychotherapist. Looking back, what I realise now is that I was teaching myself about who I was.

The more I studied, and became personally committed to the demands of various courses I enrolled in, the stronger my mind became, enjoying the challenges and demands that learning placed in my path. Anyone who has studied psychotherapy will know that much of the training involves examining closely one's own shortcomings and the dark side of nature that exists within each of us – a side that very few of us are ever keen to even acknowledge. However, this dark side is as much a part of each of us as the person we prefer others to see; so without shining a light on it, and recognising it for what it is and what role it might play in our lives, as a psychotherapist you can't possibly hope to offer support to a patient who comes to see you for help.

A client (or patient) who makes an appointment

to see a psychotherapist is doing so because, possibly unknown to themselves, they are concerned that 'the shadow' within them is causing a major imbalance in their lives. Unless therapists have faced their own 'shadow' and are familiar and comfortable with working with issues that relate to their client's shadow, they won't be able to offer the support their client needs as therapist and client together examine the deep inner workings of the troubled mind. Swiss psychiatrist Carl Jung first used the term 'shadow' to describe our dark side – that sinister part of our personality that is kept hidden from our ego. Throughout our lives we carefully choose and design and become the type of person we want other people to believe is 'the real me', but on some rare occasions, the shadow breaks through, revealing a side of us that is both uncomfortable and unattractive, and completely at odds with the public ego that most people see.

In order to be a strong and balanced therapist, I had to face up to my own misgivings and past shortcomings, because a therapy session is the last place you want to be dwelling on your own feelings of doubt about the problem your client is telling you about. Of course it's not always that straightforward. Therapists are as human and as vulnerable as the clients who come to see them. But that's essentially what makes the connection between therapist and patient work.

One major assignment I was set was to write ten thousand words (about thirty pages) on the question, 'Does being personally flawed lend towards greater empathy to others?' It was a challenging essay to complete. The question could be reworded as: 'How can I possibly believe I can help someone else when there are times I can't even help myself?'

We are all flawed, most likely in many ways and at different levels – mentally, spiritually, emotionally and psychologically. Many people think that by studying psychotherapy, you are transformed into the perfect human being. You know everything and can therefore resolve any problem you're faced with. Not true. In fact, studying psychotherapy made me realise just how vulnerable a person I was, and still am. It also taught me that the only way I can learn more about who I am and for what purpose I am here is by listening intently to what those who came to see me tell me about themselves and their lives. On some occasions, clients turned the tables and started asking me questions. One rather stubborn client asked me, 'What makes you think you can make all my problems go away?' To which I replied, 'I was hoping you could tell me the answer to that.'

While I no longer practise as a therapist, I look back on the many hours I have spent supporting people while they painstakingly and bravely picked through the pieces of their broken lives, attempting to set in place the makings of a new life that could help them to move forward. No one wants to go backwards. Clients would tell me at the start of our first session, 'I just want my old life back.' To which I would reply, 'Why do you want your old life back? Sure isn't that where all the issues and all the problems started? Why don't we focus on making something brand new? You can have your old life back right now if you want. All you have to do is stand up and walk out the door and don't come back.' It worked every time.

I practised as a therapist for almost ten years, mostly in a part-time capacity, as I continued to present my afternoon radio show Monday to Friday. So many wonderful people come to mind whenever I think back to 'the rooms', as I often called the offices where I practised. The tears, anger, laughter, disbelief, acceptance ... and then the moments when the air was suddenly tense with the realisation that the person sitting before me was reaching the end of their ordeal, finding their way out of their darkness; after so much soul-searching they were finally arriving at a place they might have experienced for the first time in their lives, called self-actualisation. They were finally able to shake off the burden that had left them searching for peace for many years from the emotional pain.

I have mostly happy memories of those sessions I felt privileged to be part of. It's never easy to sit in front of a stranger and try to help them unravel the complicated path their life journey might have taken. Life is like a maze where no one gets out alive. So the best we can hope for is to navigate the maze in such a way that we avoid getting lost as much as possible. A therapist I knew many years ago told a conference I was a guest at that he believed we all are ultimately responsible for creating whatever problems and anxieties confront us in life, because we set our lives up in such a way that we leave ourselves exposed to hurt and pain. I stood up and disagreed with him as soon as he said it. 'Do you mean to tell me that victims of domestic abuse and violence, victims of rape, victims of child sexual abuse set themselves up to be hurt?' I could tell that many people in the audience were both deeply offended and angered by the speaker's comments. He has since passed away. I think the point he was trying to make was that often we place too much trust in other people when we shouldn't, because we don't know enough about them to trust them so quickly. Emotions are very powerful triggers. Too often we take a leap of faith because we act on a feeling, but it turns out to be a bad mistake. It's called life. Most of the time we can't account for what lies ahead, which is probably why fortune tellers will never be unemployed.

'Once a therapist, always a therapist,' a friend of mine reminds me whenever he thinks I'm analysing a conversation we're having. I guess there is a ring of truth to what he says. Becoming a therapist makes you more aware of your own needs. We have the tools we need to help others, but we rarely use them on ourselves. Becoming a therapist didn't make me superhuman; it simply reminded me that by taking ownership of my own vulnerability I was more aware of how vulnerable others were when they came to me looking for help. We are all 'a bit neurotic'. A neurotic behaviour is an automatic, unconscious effort to manage deep anxiety. Yes I am a bit neurotic, and also eccentric in a gentle sort of way. Perhaps that's because I can become quite anxious over even the smallest things. I have learned to accept these personality traits as part of who I am. What you see is what you get.

During my time in practice, I learned that therapists can become deeply depressed, as I did on more than one occasion, and most likely will again. They can feel the deepest anxiety when they least expect to, as I often do. I also learned that none of my psychology training would help me to deal with the initial shock and the consequent dark pit of depression I fell into after learning of my own life-changing diagnosis in 2018.

However, by witnessing the inner strength of some of those people who came to talk to me about their own life-threatening situations, and then to have watched hope grow within them as they found their way out of their darkness, I like to believe that I have been able to find the strength and the hope I need to continue on my own journey for as long as I can.

Chapter 6

OUT OF A CLEAR BLUE SKY: SEPTEMBER 2001

A passenger plane had crashed into the North Tower of the World Trade Center in New York. It was one of those moments where you instinctively feel the need to grab your phone and call someone, anyone, just to be able to share what you have seen. But I couldn't phone anyone.

I recoiled in my chair and my headphones toppled sideways off my head as I watched the giant aircraft slam into the huge skyscraper and disappear inside. It was as if the building had just swallowed it in one mouthful, belching out an enormous mushroom shape of red and orange flame with grey and white smoke on all sides, turning into a pitch-black storm cloud within seconds, debris and wreckage raining down the sides of the ruptured building onto the streets of Manhattan as the city prepared to go to work that morning.

My heart was pounding as I realised that what I was watching on the screen in front of me was actually happening in real time. And the television wasn't in the corner of my living room at home, but mounted in the radio studio directly in front of me.

I thought back to the streets around the World Trade Center where I had strolled less than a year before on a sunny morning just like this one – the coffee shops and book stores I had fallen in love with, and the traffic, noise and bustle of New York City, with its hundreds of accents and its unique atmosphere. For a moment I was back there, reliving the heartbeat of a city I love dearly. That city was under attack that morning, but on a scale my mind could not comprehend.

All I could do was stare at the screen. In a studio that should have been a hive of activity ahead of my three-hour radio show, time was standing still. It was as if nothing else mattered except what was unfolding on the screen in front of me. My eyes felt salty and sore. Suddenly I wanted to be at home with my family, to be there for my young daughters, reassuring them that we were safe, offering some kind of explanation; but we were anything but safe, from what I could see of the horror unfolding on the screen in front of me. And there was no explanation I could think of.

John Kenny's familiar voice opposite me was audible but seemed more at a distance now than before, as if it was coming from the room next door. And then came an abrupt silence.

The sports bulletin had ended. John was staring at me. 'I've finished!' he said in a joking tone. At that point I was supposed to thank him, engage in some witty, light-hearted banter and then hit the jingle to start my radio show, just as I had done every afternoon for what felt like forever. But that afternoon I couldn't do any of these things.

We were live on air. It was 2.05 p.m. on a beautiful sunny Tuesday afternoon in September 2001. It should have been just another random weekday afternoon show, no different from the previous afternoon, or any other afternoon in the previous weeks or months. I remember it as if it were yesterday; I can even recall how blue the sky was in Dublin that day.

Earlier, as I sat on the steps outside the radio station, taking in some fresh air and warm sunshine before I started the show, I had even pointed to the white lines of the transatlantic jetliners that were crossing above our heads, heading west at tens of thousands of feet. It was something I often did; depending on who was sitting with me, we would sometimes try to figure out if it was a four-engine Boeing, or a two-engine Airbus. Most days, it passed ten minutes before we headed into the studio for that day's show.

I had lined up my usual type of show: a couple of guests due to call into studio; friendly chat and lots of music. Little did I know that the next three hours would have a more profound effect on me than I could ever have imagined. I flicked to PFL (pre-fade listen) on the studio desk which allowed me to listen to live coverage of the television news programme. It was CNN's morning show. The two presenters were trying to get clarification on what had just happened. There was panic and fear in their voices. One of them confirmed that a plane had indeed crashed into the North Tower. I flicked off the PFL, and reverted to my own studio feed. There was silence.

John Kenny was still looking at me askance, willing me to fill the ever-growing silence. 'A passenger plane has just crashed into the World Trade Center,' I finally said, as I looked back at him. I think they were my exact words. I remember leaning towards the television screen to get a better view. At first, John seemed to think it was some sort of cruel joke, but when I pointed to the screen, I could hear him say 'Oh my God'.

Radio studios tend to be calm, quiet places. It would have been easy to forget there were a quarter of a million listeners beyond those walls waiting to hear what I was about to say next. At this point during a normal show there would be music playing, and I would be preparing to tell my audience which guests were lined up to join me later in the afternoon.

All that seemed completely irrelevant now. There was no music, just an ever-louder silence in the studio. I quickly decided there would be no guests. I knew my microphone was still switched on and I was going to have to decide within the next few seconds of silence how I was going to explain the events that were unfolding in front of my eyes.

I could actually hear the beating of my heart in the microphone – and if that was the case, so, I knew, could the listeners. In one ear of my headphones I was listening to the CNN commentators giving live updates on details that they were getting. As they were speaking, I was in turn trying to repeat what they were telling their viewers to my listeners.

Then suddenly all hell broke loose. There was a second plane approaching the World Trade Center. It was flying low, silhouetted against the crystal-clear morning sky. I watched in horror as it tipped its wings to the left, completed a U-turn and then appeared to accelerate, its nose pointed directly at the mid-section of the South Tower. I remember hearing myself saying, 'I'm watching a second plane heading for the South Tower; it is on a collision course.'

Now my voice started to quiver as I spoke into the microphone, trying to describe what was happening at the point of impact. Again, the plane seemed to crash through the side of the building and then there was a massive explosion. Followed by another huge explosion that blew out a portion of the tower on the opposite side that I remember expecting the plane to exit through. But it didn't.

As I continued to give details, I looked to my left through the glass window that separated the studio from the control room; Jim Lockhart, my producer, was now being joined by producers and researchers from other radio shows. As I talked while reminding myself to slow down and not to wander off on any loose tangents, I waved to Jim in order to attract his attention. He flicked a switch which gave him access to my headphones. I could now hear his voice, which was a huge comfort to me.

'Keep it going, keep on talking. You're doing fine, Gareth. We're lining up some people who are in Manhattan for you to talk to. Conor O'Clery from *The Irish Times* should be on line two in a few seconds. Take a commercial break and give out the text number and the email address; tell listeners to stay with us, that we'll be back in two minutes.'

Just before taking a break as Jim had suggested, I explained again briefly to everyone listening what had just happened in New York. Little did any of us know that this was just the beginning.

As the commercials ran, I looked at the text screen to my left. Text messages were coming in so fast it was difficult to keep up with them. Further to my left, I saw two polystyrene cups of coffee sitting on the desk. I had no idea where they came from, but I drank them both in the time I had left in the ad break.

Then we were back live on air. I looked at the clock. It was almost 2.30 p.m. (9.30 a.m., New York time). We were only half an hour into the show but it felt as though I had been talking for hours.

For the next two and a half hours I continued to describe each heartbreaking development as it happened. We spoke to people who were listening online in Manhattan, some not far from the World Trade Center. I read out many texts from Irish people living in and visiting New York, all hoping to reach their families and loved ones here at home through the radio show, to reassure them that they were safe.

Somewhere during the bewildering confusion of

that afternoon, I told listeners about the strike on the Pentagon. I told them about a fourth passenger plane that was unaccounted for at that point, and which authorities suspected was destined to strike the White House. It just felt as though it was never going to end. I still remember the sound of sheer horror in my voice as I described how the towers were collapsing live on a screen in front of me. And just when it felt as though I had no more energy left to give, we received news that a passenger plane had crashed into a remote field in Pennsylvania.

Before I realised it, it was almost 5 p.m., almost time to say goodbye to the listeners. Time had entered another dimension that afternoon. It felt as though we had all been sucked up into a violent tornado, then suddenly it all seemed to stop. Many were dead, many didn't know if they were going to die or live, while others just couldn't find words to describe how it felt to have survived.

In the few minutes left before the scheduled news bulletin after my show, it was decided that I should play a song rather than just leaving the studio on an abrupt farewell. There just seemed to be nothing left for me to say, no gentle words to end on. So, as I gave out some emergency phone numbers for families and loved ones who were concerned for those they couldn't contact in New York that afternoon, the first chords of Don Henley's 'New York Minute' began to play with an unbearable poignancy as I thanked the team who had supported me, and without whom I would not have got through those three hours.

All these years later, of all the footage I watched that afternoon, there are two intensely vivid moments that stay in my mind, as if they had happened only yesterday. The devastating image of the immaculately dressed man as he dropped head-first in freefall from one of the windows high above where one of the planes had struck is etched deep in my memory and shocks me to this day. His white shirt was billowing in the wind; I saw him hurtling through the air, his arms by his side; his left leg was bent at an angle, its foot pressed against his right knee. Upside down, he fell faster and faster until he disappeared.

Nor will I ever forget the tragic image of Fr Mychal Judge, dead and broken, being carried in a chair by four devastated firefighters. Fr Mychal was a chaplain to the New York City Fire Department; he joined his firefighter colleagues as they ran into the lobby of the North Tower where an emergency command post had been set up. There he stayed, offering support and prayers for the rescuers, the injured and the dead. When the South Tower collapsed, debris flew through the North Tower lobby, killing Fr Judge. He would become the first certified fatality of the 11th of September attacks.

Perhaps one of the reasons why, even in recent times, I never seem to be far from the events of 9/11 is because of the huge personal impact they had on me. It might have been different if I had been sitting in an office with colleagues, or at home watching a television set, listening to a commentator updating me as each minute unfolded. Instead I became that commentator, and not by choice. I just happened to be sitting in my studio about to go on air when it all suddenly kicked off. There could never have been any kind of preparation possible, because no one with a conscience would ever have believed, let alone imagined, that such a devastating, concerted attack could happen with such ease.

In the years since then I have read many books about 9/11, watched many documentaries, cried during many anniversary tributes and of course listened with intrigue to many of the so-called conspiracy theories about what 'really' happened that day, a number of which have garnered huge support.

In 2019, on the eighteenth anniversary of the attacks, first responders once again called on the US Congress to reopen the 9/11 investigation. There have been consistent demands from one branch of the New York Fire Department (NYFD) involved in the rescue efforts that day for a new congressional inquiry. They are currently attempting to gather the support of the entire fire service in New York State to put pressure on Congress to reopen the investigation. Such a call would seem to me to be extremely newsworthy for the US networks which regularly remind us to 'never forget'; however, this demand for a new inquiry by a senior-ranking member of the NYFD was met with total silence from the mainstream media.

Asking any awkward questions about the official

conclusions of the first federal investigation into the attacks appears to be taboo among the American media, although it's worth noting here that even those who fronted the commission say the investigation was 'set up to fail' from the start, and they were repeatedly lied to and deceived by federal officials in relation to the events of the day.

A book I recommend to those who might wonder what it must have been like to be one of the ordinary men and women who became caught up in the unthinkable nightmare of that day is Garrett M. Graff's *The Only Plane in the Sky: The Oral History of 9/11*. Like no other, Graff's masterful exploration skilfully tells the story of the unfolding events as they were lived through from never-before-published transcripts, archived interviews, and from the accounts and stories of hundreds of people who together weave a devastating jigsaw of profound humanity as they struggled to cope with a single day that changed not just the course of history, but all of our lives. I have read many books about 9/11, but this book in its unique way brought me into the presence of something so private and sacred that even the voice of my heart had changed by the time I was finished reading it.

As I slowly walked through the deserted open-plan office of the radio station that evening, I became aware that a phone was ringing somewhere in a distant corner. I had a splitting headache, and all I wanted was to get to the front entrance for some badly needed fresh air, back to where I had been sitting that afternoon, ten minutes before my show started, watching those distant planes crossing the skies high above us. I wanted to get away from the studio and the radio station, as far and as fast as I possibly could. I felt this compelling urge to run away from the madness of the last three hours and never come back.

The phone kept ringing. I tried to ignore it and kept walking. But then I stopped, thinking it might be important to someone, somewhere out there on that awful evening, that I answer it. Eventually I located it, underneath a pile of morning newspapers, bearing the headlines and stories of the previous day that few would ever remember now.

I dropped my bag to the ground and picked up the receiver.

'Hello,' I said. My voice felt dry and raw, and my throat was sore. I waited.

Then the soft, hesitant voice of a woman who was clearly distressed spoke to me. 'I'm sorry for calling so late, but I didn't know where else to call.'

I could hear the pain and upset in her voice. 'That's okay. It's not late at all. How can I help you?'

She recognised my voice. 'Is that you, Gareth?' Her words suddenly sounded brighter. For a moment I thought she sounded like my mother.

'It is,' I said, and sat down. I drew the chair in closer to the desk and steadied my elbows for support.

'I'm so glad I got to talk to you; I've been listening to your show all afternoon.'

There was a long silence, until I realised she was crying. 'Has something happened?' I asked.

'It's my daughter, Caroline. I've been trying to call her all day but I can't get an answer. Her phone is ringing, but it just goes to her voicemail. It's very odd that she doesn't call me back within a few minutes.'

'Where is Caroline?'

'New York. She works in Manhattan. I've been trying to phone her office phone number ever since you told us what was happening.'

'Many of the phone services are down in New York this evening. Maybe she has been trying to contact you, to let you know she's okay. Maybe she's been trying as often as you have.'

I was aware of the strong scent of women's perfume on the phone I was holding. It reminded me how in moments of extreme tragedy and loss, our senses become so heightened. A perfume indelibly marked on a phone carrying a conversation of desperation between two total strangers; a scent which forever marked that conversation in my mind.

'Maybe you should take a short break, perhaps get yourself something to eat? You need to stay strong for your daughter, because she'll naturally be worrying about you too.' I was hoping my words were helping. 'Have you anyone at home with you?'

'No,' she replied. 'I'm on my own since Caroline went to New York.'

'When did she go?' I asked, trying to keep the conversation going.

'Two weeks ago – she started a new job yesterday.' She paused a moment. 'Yesterday was Monday, wasn't it?'

I was about to say 'yes', when she continued: 'Thank you so much for taking my call. It must have been very difficult, talking about all those poor, unfortunate people dying this afternoon. I hope you are not on your own this evening.' They were her last words. Most phones were not equipped with a redial facility back then, and so I had no way of calling her back.

For weeks afterwards, I checked each day on arriving into work to see if she had called back and perhaps left a message. But she never did. I can only hope that she got through to her daughter eventually – and that Caroline was safe.

I remember thinking while I lay in bed that night that someone was turning a key in a hall door at that precise moment, placing the key on a hall table and calling out a loved one's name; hearing no reply, and then calling again.

For many of those who were walking into their hallways or their apartments, they simply assumed that the city was in lockdown, that dinner would be late tonight, that they would lie in bed together later in the night unable to sleep, grateful to be able to share their stories of that terrifying day, to be finally holding each other tightly, thankful to be alive and lying in each other's arms.

He calls her name again, this time louder, just to be sure. No answer. Then he notices the red light on the answering machine beside the phone is flashing. There's just one message.

Was that the moment that many people realised that their loved ones would never be coming home again? A woman walks into a bedroom and finds the bed unmade and a message on the pillow saying, 'We'll order in this evening … pizza and wine maybe? I love you.' A man walks into a kitchen and finds a message that says, 'I'll collect the kids from crèche.

See you later. I love you.' But there's no one home. They're never this late.

We would find out later that most messages left on people's voicemails that day were the words 'I love you.' For so many, it was the last time they would ever hear them.

No doubt some of you reading this are wondering, 'Why write an entire chapter about a series of events that took place twenty years ago?' I have so many answers to that question; so let me distil them and see if I can explain. 9/11 changed my entire view of the world. If ever I had a sense of being in this life before the events of that day, then that state of mind collapsed with those towers. I suddenly felt somewhere on the outside of life. It was a tragedy of such infinite proportions I just couldn't get my head around it. I still can't; even when we visited New York in 2019, the devastation of 9/11 still hung in the Manhattan air like a layer of sadness that never lifts. The message throughout Don Henley's classic song 'New York Minute' is about having and showing appreciation for the things we have. It's a song about how quickly and how cruelly life can be changed forever. Everything we regard as precious and personal can disappear in the blink of an eye. I often play the song, listening closely to the words set against Jai Winding's keyboard playing, whenever I'm reminded that my own diagnosis is also something that has left me on the outside of life. Most of us live our lives as though we are never going to die. Of course this is only natural. However, that inbuilt unconscious sense of unending existence came to an abrupt stop for me when I was told I had a very serious illness that will never go away.

I sometimes think of the people who were trapped in those towers that morning, on those floors that were high above the crash zones, their fates sealed by the intense heat and smoke and fumes which made their escapes impossible. Did they cry? Did they argue? Did someone assume the role of leader and try to calm work colleagues? Did they pray out loud? Did they perhaps sing a hymn – just like many of the passengers on board the *Titanic* did in those final moments – as they knew there were only seconds left until the huge buildings groaned and finally gave up their strength?

I sometimes contemplate what they might have been thinking. I expect most of them realised their fate. They were already transiting between life and death, being drawn further away from the routinely typical lives they woke up to that morning, lives that were imbued with normality; with purpose, feelings, priorities and rush-hour frustrations as they made their way to work.

For those who lost loved ones on 9/11, tragedy stole away all familiar meaning of purpose and attachment. It becomes a 'one day at a time' struggle, until something – we're never sure what that's going to be – quietly speaks to your heart and says, 'It will never be fully gone, but it's important to move on.' I never believed for a moment, during that long 9/11 broadcast, that I would end up fighting every day to stay strong and to remain as healthy as I can be, when I watch how this disgusting disease tries to steal a little more away from all that I love. Perhaps that's why 9/11 deserves its own chapter here, as a tribute to those who never came home, and especially those who to this day struggle silently to stay strong and to find purpose and meaning in this unpredictable setting we call life.

When I look back over the day and I know that those I love are well, that I've done the best I can, and that I am thankful for all I have – that's all that really matters.

Chapter 7

BREAKING THE SILENCE

I was invited to host the annual conference of the mental health organisation Aware during the spring of 2002. At first I was reluctant to do it, as my own experience with depression was still a closely guarded secret. I didn't want anyone to know that I had been diagnosed with it. The last thing I needed was unwanted attention from people I didn't know. I was finding it difficult enough to cope with my own feelings, without courting publicity and the ensuing media attention that I had no doubt would be focused on me if the news got out. It's worth remembering that in 2002, the term 'mental health' had yet to be coined. Depression was still known as a mental illness.

Eventually I agreed to host the event. However, the day before the conference, my phone rang. The organisers had just received a message from their keynote speaker who lived in London to say that she wasn't feeling well and had been advised by her doctor not to travel. More than four hundred guests were expected to attend, and now there was the challenge of trying to find a noteworthy speaker to address them. I knew what was coming next.

'Will you be our keynote speaker, Gareth?' the CEO asked me.

'I can't, sorry.'

'Well, then, we'll have to cancel the conference ...'

'Why can't you or one of your colleagues be the keynote speaker?'

'No one knows who I am; the same goes for them.'

There was a long silence as I considered the situation. 'Okay,' I finally said, 'I'll do it.'

I spent most of the night wide awake, regretting that I had agreed to speak. Now I was going to turn up at the conference exhausted. It would be a complete shambles. I also knew that by standing up in front of four hundred people, admitting I suffered from depression and telling my story, I was going public and there would be no way back from that.

The following day, when introduced on stage, I received an enormously warm welcome from the audience. I then spoke for an hour, forgetting completely about the scribbled notes I had made in the early hours of the morning, having realised that honesty was the only option if I wanted to relate my experiences in a way that might help others. As I continued to speak, I watched as people in the audience wiped away tears and appeared to be nodding in agreement with what I was saying. I received a standing ovation. I had never experienced a feeling quite like it, but I also knew that there were quite a few journalists in that large audience, and that it was only a matter of days before everyone knew my story.

The following week, I was a guest on *The Marian*

Finucane Show on RTÉ Radio 1. Marian had read about the conference in her local newspaper and had called me at home the day after the event, with an invitation to chat to her on her show. Almost half a million people were listening that morning, and the following day I ended up on the front page of every newspaper. As I left the studio after the interview, Marian followed me out into the hallway to thank me. 'You have lifted the lid on something very important here, something that needed to be spoken about to as wide an audience as possible, and that lid will never go back on again,' she said. And she was right.

Out of that interview came the idea for *A Day Called Hope*. It was published exactly one year later, in 2003, and became one of the biggest-selling books in Ireland at the time. I still receive emails from people who are either trying to find a copy of the book, or who have read it and want to let me know how my story helped them on their own personal journeys. As a result of the success of the book, I received countless invitations to give talks at conferences and to community groups and local clubs across the country. I never once refused an invitation to speak about depression, as I understood how important it was to support those who were going through what I had been through, as well as to break down the taboos, and by doing so help others recognise that to admit you are depressed is not a sign of weakness, but rather a sign of strength.

A Day Called Hope described my personal journey through and beyond a long period of depression that rocked my life for years. In order to understand it, I had to educate myself as to what depression meant to me; but there was no one around to educate me. So the book became my personal account of what I believed was happening to me based on how it was making me feel. It found its way into bookshops around the world, including China, Greece, Portugal, France and Croatia. One elderly man sent me a beautiful handwritten letter from his home in Croatia, describing how my book had given him hope and strength as he continued to mourn the loss of his sons, his grandson and his brother in the Serbian-Croatian war. They had been rounded up by members of the Serbian army early one morning and taken in trucks to the local town square, which was full of local men of all ages, including children as young as his grandson. The children were given sweets by the soldiers to keep them quiet. No one quite knew what was going on until large army trucks arrived at the edge of the town square. Soldiers closed off all side streets and avenues and all of the men and children were loaded into the trucks and taken to a remote field where they were executed by firing squad.

I cried as I read his letter that night. I kept it in my work case for weeks afterwards, taking it out of its envelope and re-reading it over and over, intending to try to find the words to reply to him. It's one of my great regrets that I never did.

It took me a very long time to come to terms with the enormous success and public reaction to my book, and the profound effects I was told it had on the lives of so many people. I could never have known in advance just how sought-after the book would become, and I reached a point in my life where I became consumed by it. Or perhaps it consumed me. It was as though for almost two years after its publication the book became me and took over every aspect of my life. Of course I have never once

Gareth O'Callaghan

regretted writing *A Day Called Hope*. I am humbled to this day that so many people found a sense of healing and personal belonging in the words that filled its pages. In hindsight I think I was also shocked by the amount of 'hidden' depression that appeared to be everywhere, but yet nowhere; in the sense that many people were suffering pain that they could never openly talk about, because to do so would have been seen as a weakness. So the majority endured their pain in silence, in order to avoid bringing undue attention upon themselves. It's not so long ago that depression was seen as a curse within a family. In some corners of our modern society, little has changed.

But I was battling my own demons. Writing my story left me yet again facing the painful truth of my own experiences. It shook my life to its very core. It was as if I had stepped into the path of a tornado. I had thought that by committing everything to paper, I would finally be setting the pain of my past aside. Instead it had come roaring back, worse than ever. Of course it hadn't gone away. Maybe it never will go away. Could depression be something that I will have to learn to live with for the rest of my life? Perhaps that's what Marian Finucane meant when she talked to me after the interview. Perhaps she was referring to my own life, and not just my decision to 'go public' about my depression.

I was forced to confront the truth that the life I had been living could not continue the way it was going. I was being asked to give talks and attend conferences. I was visiting colleges and schools to chat with students about the need to discuss emotions and the benefits of sharing the anxiety that might be making life impossible to bear. But you can't stand up in front of a group of vulnerable people who have come to listen to you in the hope that you can be instrumental in changing their lives for the better, when behind the scenes your own life is a crumbling mess.

I spoke earlier about our reluctance to let go of the past. It's almost as if we won't survive if we let go of all that happened in our lives before now, even the nasty stuff that really hurt us. There are lots of people who can't let go of the pain of the past, even though it will end up making them ill. As I have personally learned, your past will continue to put your life on hold if you are constantly looking back at it; then your past becomes your future, and nothing changes because you become stuck in the present. It's a complete mess. It's exactly how my life was for so long. There are too many people urging me these days to live in the present moment. People have made millions out of mindfulness and meditation, both very useful exercises if they appeal to you. But I'm not interested in living in the present moment. I want to move on quickly with my life. I want to close the door on the past. I have a strong purpose.

Of course it's often not so easy to simply close a door on the past. Often there are times from the past that still haunt us; deep within the unconscious mind painful experiences prevent us from letting go. I mentioned in Chapter 4 that I had been sexually abused as a young boy. Over the years since then I really believed that I had moved beyond these experiences and the pain they had caused me for so long. I never realised there was still a darkness that had remained almost hidden from conscious memory so long after the actual events, a darkness that tapped me on the shoulder briefly as if to remind me it was still there following my visit to the psychologist in 2001.

It was early 2005 when those terrifying memories quite unexpectedly came to life again, with almost devastating consequences. I had invited an old friend, Don Baker, to join me on my afternoon show to chat and perform a couple of songs from his new album. Don is a great musician and entertainer, and is unsurpassed when it comes to the harmonica. He brings it to life like no one else I have ever heard. He has also appeared in several films, the most notable being *In the Name of the Father* where he played IRA prisoner Joe McAndrew. In addition to his many other talents, Don is a brilliant storyteller. During our live interview that afternoon, I asked him to talk about his time at St Conleth's Reformatory School in Daingean, County Offaly; I knew he had been incarcerated there as a young boy for some minor offences he had committed.

However, none of us listening to Don as he spoke about his time in Daingean was expecting what happened next. Suddenly he began to relate the graphic details of the abuse and savage beatings which had been dealt out to the young boys who were sent there, including himself. At one point during the interview he broke down and wept. I couldn't speak because I was so shocked by what Don was telling me, it felt as if there were just no words to say. All I could do was look out into the control room at my team, who were also visibly upset.

The interview made it into the following morning's newspapers. Don's revelations became the subject of discussion all over the country, long after the day of the broadcast. The whole issue of institutional abuse, which was rarely out of the news headlines then, was once again splashed across the front pages. While a couple of senior management personnel at the station were highly critical, claiming that such a topic was not suitable for my show or for the time of day, the reaction from listeners was overwhelmingly supportive of Don and his bravery for being so honest. One listener texted: 'You have no idea how many people you have helped today; you have most likely saved lives by giving hope, by proving there is life after abuse. Thank you.'

St Conleth's was one of the many schools investigated by the Ryan Commission, chaired by Mr Justice Sean Ryan, which published its report in 2009. I like to think that Don Baker's radio interview that afternoon lent a solid voice to many of the young boys who disappeared during their incarceration in Daingean. I am sure the lush green banks of the Grand Canal running alongside what once were the walls of St Conleth's could tell a few shocking secrets.

In the aftermath of that interview, my own abuse started to haunt me – to devastating effect, as we will see. I have no doubt that this long-buried trauma was shaken awake somewhere in my unconscious mind by Don's words. It would be impossible not to have been deeply affected by the anger and poignancy of his testimony, in all its bare, bitter truth.

Chapter 8

ABUSE IN THE SHADOWS

When I was a young teenager, obsessive compulsive disorder plagued my life. From the moment I woke every morning until I fell asleep exhausted at night, days which should have been carefree were filled with obsessions and compulsions that I had become a slave to. Tapping, checking and washing had all become separate rituals that criss-crossed and connected with each other. There were specific rituals to be carried out in the afternoons as soon as I arrived home from school which almost shut down my life and eventually pushed me to the point where I believed that suicide was the only option left to stop this invisible pain that I was feeling inside me all the time – a pain no one else knew about.

Eventually the pain and the anger became too much to hide any longer, so I told my mother what had happened to me. I was barely fifteen. She was shocked to the core and looked almost broken. I had never seen my mother upset before, but that day she put her arm around my shoulder and assured me that what had happened was in the past, and it could never harm me again. The sheer relief of having shared my experience with her gave me back a love for life that I thought I had lost forever – even as a young boy with such little life experience. The OCD stopped, literally overnight, and the shame I felt lifted gradually over a few weeks. But there are different levels to the scars of abuse. Some of them heal quickly, but deep down there are the indelible marks that are never fully purged, that I know now last for life.

Something that had happened to me as a small

boy – a painful secret I thought might just eventually go away – couldn't be erased by the passage of time. I slowly came to realise this as the years went by. Instead it just left a part of my soul frozen in time, in an invisible set of picture frames in a place that lives on in your head like a reality that no one else can see or visit. Many of the people in these images are long dead, their towering adult bodies reduced to a small pile of dirty bones in a forgotten grave; but in that place in your head they live on and they never die. They never even grow old. You want to move on, to know for certain there's no need to look behind you because there's no one there – but your life has become stuck in that place because it is your reality and it replays itself even though you beg it to stop, with a fear that feels as real as it did when the painful secret first became your burden to bear. It was visited on you to keep alive forever. Of course when you look behind you, there's no one there; but the fear never leaves you. That's because it's still alive inside you after all these years, like a virus that even the doctor can't see.

There is a song I remember so well from those

darker years. It is called 'Suffer Little Children'; to this day it still has the ability to turn me into a terrified eleven-year-old boy again. A hymn recorded by the Scottish tenor Canon Sydney MacEwan and the Cork Children's Choir, it was taken from an album called *The Mass of St Francis of Assisi*. I can still remember this song being played over and over on the radio. It was so popular it made it to number one in the Irish Top Twenty music charts in 1972. 'Suffer Little Children' was even performed by our local church choir, as it was by church choirs all around the country at that time.

I had my own very personal reasons for hating the song so much. Around the time it was enjoying such fame and popularity, I was being sexually abused while on a scouting holiday at a religious order's training college. I will never be able to understand how a priest could sing about how God cares for the plight of children, while children were suffering appalling abuse at the hands of 'men and women of the cloth' all over Ireland and beyond.

The song's title is taken from St Mark's Gospel, spoken by Jesus. The word 'suffer' is used here in its archaic form, meaning 'let them', or 'allow them', and not in the literal meaning of 'suffer'; but I still hated it. Every time I heard it on our kitchen radio I would lock myself in the bathroom. I was suffering horribly.

There were no victims shouting their sickening experiences from the rooftops back then. It was a shocking, lonely time for anyone who suffered abuse. There were no trained counsellors or therapists to help an abuse victim deal with their appalling trauma. Mostly you were on your own, if you found yourself snared by a sexual predator. Mostly you feared for your life if you dared to tell anyone what had happened to you. Victims were sworn to secrecy by their abusers. Fifty years ago, abused children who did reach out to their parents or to the local sergeant were often branded liars, usually given a stern warning never to repeat such awful accusations against such respected members of the community.

The man who abused me was a religious brother. He lived with other members of the order in a stately looking house, in Clara, County Offaly. The main residence for these brothers was attached to a secondary school and a college where young men who joined the order were trained. During the summer holidays, when the secondary school students and seminarians had gone home, the college facilities were given over to cub-scout groups and voluntary youth organisations from all over the country.

Many of the cub groups and youth clubs came from Dublin, Limerick, Galway and Cork. Some of the youth clubs were from deprived areas. While each visiting party was organised by parents and volunteers who travelled with their own groups in order to supervise them, some of the most evil predators who would remain anonymous for years to come were among the regular visitors to the summer camps.

My abuser seemed kind and funny at first. I seem to remember that he was one of the youngest members of the congregation, and was quite busy with different chores, which included looking after the older brothers and also working on the college farm. I spent my first few days learning about how to care for farm animals, and generally enjoying the freedom of the outdoors. He was inclined to spend more time working with me than with the other scouts. On a couple of occasions he even sent the others away to do various jobs in different areas of the college grounds. I remember feeling quite pleased that he wanted me to stay with him during all of the tasks he set us. Of course what I never realised at the time was that he was grooming me. I was completely taken in by him. I trusted him.

Then one night I was woken up in the pitch dark by someone shaking my shoulder. We all slept in long dormitories, each bed sectioned off by a tall, thin wooden partition. Against the moonlight that was streaming in the window, I could just about make out his shape. I could smell his aftershave. I have smelled the same scent on a number of occasions since then and it still turns my stomach and brings the memories flooding back instantly. He was standing over me. He placed his finger to his lips. 'Shush,' he whispered. 'Come with me.'

I followed him out of the dormitory, down a long hall and then up a winding staircase. It was pitch dark. He was holding a small torch by his side. He turned the key in a door that I presumed was his own bedroom and pointed to me to go inside. He checked the landing to make sure no one had seen us, then he closed the door behind him and locked it. He told me to get into the double bed, while he started to take his clothes off. He sexually abused me that night for the first time, as a wooden crucifix of Jesus on the Cross hung on the wall beside the bed, illuminated by a ghostly red night light.

Later that night he took me back to my dormitory and quickly left. The next morning I waited for him at the entrance to the small animal enclosure, like I did each of the previous mornings; but today was different. I was terrified as I couldn't comprehend in any way what had happened the night before. There were just no words that made any sense. When he saw me, he spoke to me as though nothing had happened, but there was a more distant tone in his voice. However, later that morning, I found myself alone with him while collecting hens' eggs from the large coop close to the river.

'Don't ever mention to anybody what happened last night. Do you hear me?'

His voice was different. It sounded both stern and scared. I nodded.

'Do you hear me? I'll tell them you were stealing

from my bedroom if you do. And then they will call in the local police ...'

I was terrified. I no longer trusted him, or felt comfortable being around him. I wanted to get out of my daily duties but he told me it was too late into the holiday to train up another boy. And so I had no choice but to stay. He had groomed me and now he was abusing me: an ingenious, seamless plan; a sexual predator masquerading as a religious brother, destroying the life and dreams of a small, innocent boy on a scouting holiday with his friends. After that the abuse settled into a pattern as it was repeated nightly until I left the college to return home the following week. I told no one. You couldn't. A man of God abuses a small boy. It was unthinkable. Even the word 'abuse' was unheard of back then. So I simply buried the secret. Only to discover that it would come back to me in my nightmares.

I became trapped in a web of threats and promises. He visited our family home that Christmas. He brought gifts for my parents, and for me he brought a toy bear smothered in the suffocating scent of his aftershave. It was a subtle reminder of the dirty secret he was forcing me to keep; only I would know what it meant. My parents thought that he was a lovely man. Four years later, in April 1976, after I had forced myself to explain to my mother what had happened in Clara she told me she had always suspected that he was evil: 'I always had a bad feeling about him.'

When he visited our family home that Christmas in 1972, and slept under our roof in the bedroom next to mine, I did not sleep a wink the whole night. I was terrified that at any moment I would feel the blankets being lifted in the darkness and smell the rancid stale tobacco on his breath. But he didn't leave the room he was staying in.

I must have eventually fallen into a deep sleep around dawn because when I woke up later I could hear the filthy bastard downstairs. He was chatting with my mother who was busy preparing a hearty breakfast for him, talking about baking and hurling. I checked to make sure my pyjama bottoms were still on – they were.

When I joined them in the kitchen my abuser told

me he had some great news: my mother had agreed that I could travel to Clara during the Easter holidays by train; my father would drop me to Heuston station. My abuser would collect me in Clara, and I could stay at the college for four days.

I know of many men and women who have taken their own lives as a direct result of the ongoing sexual abuse they suffered as young children at the hands of these monsters. It could have been me. There are still days when I look back, wondering how I managed to survive when they didn't. What prevented me from killing myself? And what was it that pushed them across the line?

Four months after this brother's visit to my family home, during the Easter holidays, I travelled to Clara. The abuse started again that night. On the second day of what was supposed to be a four-day stay I walked to the railway station in the early-morning darkness. The evening before, I had plotted my escape: I would wait until I was sure everyone in the big house was asleep, then I would silently let myself out through a back door in the kitchen. I managed to do this, and when I got to the station, I boarded the early train that was coming from Galway for home. I had my return ticket so there were no questions asked. I never thought I would make it as far as the station; I kept expecting at any moment to hear a car behind me in the darkness, and a voice calling my name, telling me to 'Get in!' It didn't happen. Not a single car passed me on the one-mile walk.

My mother was shocked when she opened the hall door and saw me standing there. I made the excuse that the brother had been called away due to a family emergency and so he had dropped me to the station. My mother didn't even notice that I wasn't holding the small brown suitcase I left home with. I had left it behind me in the hope that if he woke up he might think I had gone to the bathroom. I spent the remainder of the day trying to think of an excuse, of what I would say when the phone would ring, with my abuser enquiring where I had gone to. The call never came.

Over the years, I felt like my life had been split in two when I was eleven years old. That little boy was completely different and detached from all I went on to achieve in life. His life just stopped moving forward. He had been silenced by his abuser, so he didn't speak out about his shocking secret. But his secret was so crippling and overwhelming that it had a profound effect on everything in his life, tarring it black and feathering it with the suffocating memories that would randomly pop up in his dreams:

He can see himself running along the bank of a wide, fast-flowing river.

A breathless voice sounds close behind him, slowly catching up with him, shouting out his name. The voice sounds angry. The boy has never run this far before, along the bank of this river. The grassy path is becoming wet and mucky. His runners are sinking into the soft mud. If he can find a bridge, or a shallow stretch of water, he will take his chances and cross the river to a narrow road that runs alongside it. A passing car might take him to the railway station. He made sure to keep his return train ticket to Dublin in his trousers pocket that morning.

There is no one behind him now. He slows and looks back. He listens. Birds chirp and whistle; a wood pigeon coos out from the branches above. He is alone. He glances across the river – seven, maybe eight inches of shallow clear water. He can see the tiny minnows and some brown trout, but this isn't a time for fishing. He manoeuvres his way across the fast flow, from rock to stone, careful not to fall and soak his train ticket.

Minutes later he finds himself on the side of a small winding country road. There's a low, heavy cloud. The road is not familiar. He listens again for a moment, the sound of cattle somewhere in the distance. He reckons the railways station is back to the left, so he starts walking. His heart soars as he hears a car behind him slowing down.

He's about to ask the driver for a lift to the railway station. Then he feels weak and sick, with a lump in his stomach that only ever happens when he knows what lies ahead of him. His chest feels heavy as his heart beats so fast with fear. He tries to run but he can't. His feet are stuck to the ground. He can't move anything because his body has frozen. It's Him.

He leans across and opens the passenger door: 'Get in!' he says angrily.

It was the same nightmare every time, a dream that never changed its sequence of events, step by step. Once it started, it couldn't be stopped or altered in any way. Over the years it became a lucid dream. Even though I was asleep, part of my mind knew the dream had started. Somewhere in my mind, my abuser still felt like a threat. That part of me would revert to being an eleven-year-old boy frozen in time and unable to find his way out of the darkness on those nights. The little boy lived in the darkness of the past. It seemed as though there could be no future for him until the dream stopped and he could get back safely to the railway station. The predator couldn't get near the boy to hurt him during the day because he was only a child of the night who was trapped in the dark. I was no longer a child in the bright light of day; so he would wait until the early hours of darkness when he would reach out.

Hindsight is a gift – or a hindrance, depending on what it reveals to you. When I look back along my timeline, I can't put my finger on the precise point at which anxiety started to consume my life. Maybe it was the morning when I climbed the school railings and refused to come down. I was four years old. Is that too young to suffer from anxiety? Maybe the sexual abuse lit the flame and it's been simmering away somewhere inside me since I was eleven.

I am an anxious person. That is a fact. Outwardly I might appear quite calm and in control, but inside it doesn't take much for the adrenalin to kick in, then it has nowhere to go, no way of being burnt off. All my life I suppressed that anxiety. It seems as though I just kept shovelling it into some deep black hole somewhere in the recesses of my mind, as if it might just disappear. It didn't.

Chronic anxiety becomes unmanageable very quickly. Some people claim to thrive under stress, but no one thrives on anxiety. Unchecked, it slowly starts to tinker with the different systems of the body. Chronic anxiety is like a dripping tap. It doesn't matter where you are in the house, or how many doors you close to try and silence it, you are always still conscious of it. Drip, drip, drip, it never stops. Anxiety fries the tiny components in the human brain that are responsible for maintaining our ability to function. It destroys homeostasis – the body's natural state of harmony and balance. Homeostasis comes from two Latin words: *homeo*, meaning *same*, and *stasis*, which means *lack of motion*. It's a biological force that acts to preserve the 'status quo' (to keep things the way they presently are) and to restore it after it has been disturbed.

Imagine that the central nervous system is like a bundle of electrical cables moving out from the brain stem at the base of the skull, down through the spinal column, from there branching out into the peripheral nervous system, to every minuscule nerve ending throughout the entire body. In the same way that the electrical cables are surrounded by plastic tubing, the nerves and neurons that travel around the body are surrounded by a myelin sheathing to protect them from being exposed and damaged.

Chronic anxiety damages the nervous system over a sustained period of time. It affects blood pressure, heart rate, breathing, and all the subtle physiological procedures that need to work in harmony if we are to remain healthy and free of serious illness. Chronic anxiety pulls the plug on homeostasis, and over a period of time it is my strong belief that the body and brain become exposed to all sorts of chronic illnesses, including cancer, heart disease, and neurological illness. Unfortunately, by the time we are diagnosed with a chronic illness, it's often too late to undo the damage.

I often wonder if years of buried anxiety and unresolved trauma can push the body to a level where it can become incurably ill, especially when scientists and consultants cannot explain where a disease like multiple system atrophy comes from, or why some people can get the disease, while others manage to avoid it. Could something that happened almost fifty years ago, leaving an unresolved trauma of anxiety in the limbic brain, cause such an illness in later life? Or could a combination of traumas and bouts of severe anxiety over the years eventually tire out the parts of the brain that struggle to keep the body in a state of balance and harmony?

Not much is known about the effects of long-term chronic anxiety on the delicate workings of the human brain. While it is commonly known that many neurological disorders can cause chronic anxiety, most scientists believe that anxiety does not cause neurological disorders, even though it may be a major symptom of a neurological disorder. If chronic anxiety is presented as a symptom of a serious illness, which is true in my case, then surely one would be inclined to believe that the anxiety, if left unchecked for years, could have enabled such an illness to progress. It's an area of study that is still in its infancy. I do believe, however, that in years to come, scientists and neurosurgeons will discover a direct correlation between post-trauma-based sustained chronic anxiety and neurological disorders, including dementia.

Chapter 9

ONE DOOR CLOSES;
ANOTHER OPENS

In 2005, I decided to leave RTÉ. It wasn't a decision I took lightly. After seventeen years with the national broadcaster I felt I had gone as far as I could with that career. I was forty-four when I left. I could have applied for a role as producer with Radio 1, but instead I wanted to commit myself more to my work as a therapist. I was finding it increasingly difficult to combine both jobs, and I could tell I was being drawn to the therapist's chair more than I was to the radio studio.

Taking a giant leap into fulltime counselling had its uncertainties, primarily the guarantee of a steady income. Many people who need to see a psychotherapist often can't afford the cost of a series of sessions. My income was paid monthly by RTÉ as agreed in the contract I renegotiated annually; but out there in the land of new business, I would be walking away from the security of a monthly salary.

During my years at RTÉ, I fulfilled more ambitions than I could have thought possible. I met some truly inspiring and creative people who helped me see beyond what I thought were my limits, and to succeed in areas of the media that I would never have had the chance to get near if they hadn't offered me the challenges they did. Whenever I think back over my radio days, those seventeen years are without doubt the most memorable period of my time behind the microphone.

My decision to leave what was the second-most-listened-to show on 2FM was met with shock and disbelief, both by my listeners and my bosses. Over a quarter of a million listeners tuned in to my afternoon show every day: why would anyone, I was asked, want to walk away from that sort of success?

I remember Gerry Ryan pleaded with me to stay. 'For God's sake don't leave, the station will fall apart without you!' he exclaimed, waving his arms, over coffee one morning in the corner of the radio canteen. This was high praise indeed from a master of his trade, and one of the greatest broadcasters of my generation.

'Thanks, Gerry,' I replied. 'The only time this radio station would fall apart would be if you were no longer on the schedule.' As it turned out, I was right. It didn't take long after Gerry Ryan's death for the listenership figures at 2FM to plummet. The captain had left the ship.

It was my decision to leave. I wasn't pushed, nor did I leave to go to a better-paid job: I left because the time had come for me to leave. I have always believed that when enough is enough, it's time to move on. *Gareth O'Callaghan in the Afternoon* had been a national radio brand for sixteen years. That was how the major advertising agencies described it. I had given the show my best efforts consistently for all that time (allowing for the occasional diversion here and there); always searching for new ways to keep it topical, and ready to overhaul it in order to prevent it from going stale. I had known for a couple of years that it was time to move on. I wanted to leave the brand before it lost its energy and, more importantly, its respect.

It was also around this time that my marriage came to an end, in late 2005. Looking back now, I realise that couples grow apart. It's a fact of life.

There have been many books written about separation and divorce. This is not one of them. However, there's a well-known saying I swear by when it comes to getting advice on relationships, and it's this: 'Don't base your decision on the advice of those who don't have to deal with the results.'

Ireland was still luxuriating in the economic boom of the Celtic Tiger back in 2005, as it had been for ten greedy years, with its cash-rich culture and its incorrigible *Titanic* mentality. There was no one steering the ship; warning signs of a major recession were starting to ring loud, but no one was listening. Since the end of 1994, the banks had been throwing money at customers like confetti at the marriage of Greed and Affluenza. Homebuyers weren't just buying one house; they were buying three – one to live in and two to let out. At one point, Irish people were spending over a billion euro per year on overseas properties. Re-mortgaging became every bank's primary objective. You didn't even need to phone them to ask for money because they would call you.

Irish property prices were at an all-time high, so tens of thousands of people, from taxi drivers to tax inspectors, were buying up properties in Warsaw, Bulgaria, Florida, Cape Verde, The Algarve, the Costas, and even Cape Town, South Africa. If you preferred to play Monopoly with the big boys, then you could invest in new shopping malls, or soon-to-be-built leisure centres in Glasgow, Manchester or Newcastle. Of course we all know what happened. The Celtic Tiger years were great fun if you had access to money – preferably the banks' money. Then it all turned nasty very quickly. The bubble burst. Homes were lost, businesses went bust, and the luxury gated villas with their private swimming pools in the sunny Playas were repossessed. If I had remained working for RTÉ, with its monthly income, there's a strong probability I would have also gone mad spending like so many; but my reality was now a lot different.

I can vividly recall one bitterly cold and wet evening in November 2005, when I was in the process of making plans to move to Galway. I couldn't afford accommodation in Dublin, not even a comfortable apartment to rent. Ideally I wanted to find somewhere to live that was close to my daughters so that I could continue to see them most days. The wellness clinic I had been working out of since leaving RTÉ had closed its doors as its owners were unable to afford the outrageous rent and rates they were being charged. I couldn't open my own clinic because that required investment. Property prices were at an all-time high. Rented property was impossible to come by as tenants were afraid to move. The Celtic Tiger was like a never-ending piss-up once you had money. I now had no job or income, and my savings were running very low.

Galway was very accessible by motorway: it was a two-hour journey from Dublin. Rent was affordable, and I could work in a clinic there, and drive to Dublin and back comfortably in a day which meant I could see my daughters after school most days.

My initial plan was to travel to Galway city for a couple of days to find accommodation, a clinic where I could rent a room for my therapy practice, and if time allowed, catch up with some old friends. From Galway, I would drive to Clare where I had planned to surprise my old friend, Robbie, with an unexpected visit.

I had met Robbie for a catch-up barely a couple of months earlier while he was on a day trip to Dublin. By then we hadn't seen each other for over thirty years. He had told me in advance of our meeting that he had read *A Day Called Hope* and was keen to talk. Unknown to me, he had been going through a very difficult time himself. He had only recently returned from New York where he had hoped to settle down.

However, the relationship he was in hadn't worked out, so he had decided to come back home.

The last time we had seen each other, we were twelve years old with only a day between our birthdays. I stood up as soon as I saw Robbie come through the Shelbourne Hotel's famous revolving doors. We embraced and found a quiet corner to sit down together. I began by asking him what had brought him to Dublin. He explained that he was being fitted for a suit for a wedding, so he thought he would spend a few hours having a look around a few of his old familiar haunts.

We chatted for almost two hours. During the conversation, Robbie took out his copy of my book and asked me to sign it for him. The last time I had written anything for Robbie was when I was helping him finish his maths homework – something we regularly did for each other. I was devastated when he told me that he had been through so much mental pain. He had attempted to take his own life on a number of occasions and had spent weeks in hospital in the hope that his condition might improve.

From his mood that day, I gathered that not much

had changed for him. We chatted about depression, and I tried my best to explain that I believed it was a part of us that we have to try to learn from, and that we have to prevent from destroying us. Robbie's eyes reflected a deep sadness as he spoke about some of the harrowing experiences he had been through. Unfortunately our conversation was cut short after a couple of hours, as he needed to get back to the railway station.

As we parted I asked Robbie if we could keep in contact, in the hope that I could help him to lift himself out of this dark place. He seemed a little uncertain but agreed to give it a try. After he left, I had a heavy heart all evening, and kept thinking back over the conversation and the words he had been using, filled with doubt and uncertainty. That had been in the early autumn.

Now, on that dark, rainy November night as I sat in the small quiet bar of my local pub, my phone rang. It was shortly before ten. I recognised the voice straight away. It was Declan, another old school friend who had been suggesting the trip to see Robbie for some time. It was unusually late for Declan to call.

'Hello?' I said.

'Gareth – I'm sorry to be the one who has to tell you this, but Robbie is dead.' He paused. 'He finally did it. He was found yesterday.'

I just sat there with the phone to my ear. There was nothing I could say. Then I thanked Declan for calling and hung up. I did visit Galway the following weekend, just for the day, but I was too upset to drive to Clare. Robbie was gone so there was no reason for me to be there.

Our paths had parted in childhood, but I will forever be grateful that they crossed again that time in Dublin – even if it was only for the shortest time. I often think back to that first day at school, the two of us only four years old, as I watched Robbie climb the railings beside me. I didn't know who he was. As we clung to the diagonal fencing with our fingers, we stared at each other. If I hadn't climbed the railings that first school morning, I might have ended up sitting at another desk, beside another boy – and my life might not have been as enriched as it was through my childhood years because I had Robbie sitting beside me.

It would be easy for me to say that I wish he had held on just a bit longer to life, as we both had held on to those railings that morning, in the hope that we could once again give each other strength and resilience as we had back then. But the truth is that none of us knows what is going on in the heart and mind of anyone else, and it is unkind and unhelpful to think that we do.

A life without hope is like a tiny baby bird that falls from its nest before it learns how to fly. It will die a slow, lonely death. Hope is a desire that something positive will happen in the future; that desire fuels the soul's need to survive and to stay alive. Hope is as important as food if we are going to survive. Life is primarily about survival. If I lose hope, I lose my ability to dream of the future. None of us knows what the future holds, and that can be a terrifying thought.

Within a few months of receiving my diagnosis in 2018, I realised I had to start being honest with myself about my future, and the responsibility I owed both to myself and to those I love to take charge of what was happening to me. Resilience is the ability to respond and adapt. That's it in a nutshell. Without resilience we become overwhelmed. Our energy levels drop. We become depressed and hopeless.

We are not born resilient, just like the small bird that fell out of its nest, nor are we born with a supply of hope. We have to teach ourselves resilience, like a muscle of the mind that needs to be strengthened, flexed and exercised every day, and that in turn increases our ability to be more hopeful. To hope is to never stop believing that there's an outcome somewhere out there that will make your life better in some way. If I can respond and adapt to my health challenges, avoid becoming overwhelmed, and stay hopeful that all's not lost, then I will have the ability to bounce back. Without hope, there can be no purpose to life; and without a real purpose, it's impossible to bounce back. Hope and resilience are the two most important traits to be able to access in order to recover, whether that's from cancer, bereavement, a disappointing exam result, the end of a relationship – in fact anything that causes you to question the value of your life. Even with an illness that has no cure, and carries a fatal prognosis, there can still be hope and resilience – as I have found. I have no choice. I want to live, and I'll do everything in my power to stay alive. Many people believe that life owes them entitlements, as though life were a person. Life owes us nothing. We arrive with nothing, and we leave with nothing. What we do in between is entirely up to each one of us. There will always be people we know who appear to have it easier or better than we do, but we're only wasting valuable time comparing our lives to theirs.

Chapter 10

RETURNING TO CLARA

I moved to Galway in the early months of 2006. I had decided to put the therapy business on hold. I needed to get back to a situation where I could earn regular money if possible, and the best way to do that was by getting back into radio. By June that year I was behind the microphone once again, on Galway Bay FM's breakfast show, having been offered the position by a good friend of mine, Keith Finnegan, who runs the successful station. What started out as some temporary fill-in work turned into a fulltime contract, and I continued to work for the station until November 2008.

During my time in Galway, I commuted three times a week to see my daughters in Dublin, setting out in the car each morning as soon as I had finished the breakfast show so that I would arrive just in time to have a slice of toast and a cup of tea with my parents, before meeting my girls in the afternoon after they had finished school. By then, Kerri was seventeen and almost finished secondary school, Katie was fifteen, and Aibhín was nine and still in primary school. I usually stayed in a local B & B at weekends in order to spend as much time as possible with them. During the working week it was usually a quick return journey each day, even if it meant I only got to see them for an hour or two.

I enjoyed Galway very much, with its rich cultural heritage, its relaxed atmosphere, and its close-knit community. In the thirty minutes it would take to walk briskly from one side of the city to the other, I could witness some of Ireland's most historic landmarks.

An hour-long ramble through the beautiful cobbled side streets of the City of the Tribes on a calm, sunny Saturday morning was to bear witness to nine hundred years of history, marked by its famous ancient families and its traditional pageants and events.

Perhaps because you are always reminded of the past when in this wonderful city, it was while I was in Galway that I began to find myself dwelling on the very painful time in my own past I described in Chapter 8. The grim reminders of that time, rather than receding or fading away, increasingly began to occupy my days and nights until soon I could bear it no longer.

Whatever had happened to me during my radio interview with Don Baker three years earlier, when he spoke of the abuse he had suffered and witnessed during his time in St Conleth's, it had stirred up some very difficult personal memories that I thought I had consigned to the past. Of course it wasn't Don's fault. I am eternally grateful to him for speaking the way he did that afternoon, because his strength and resilience helped so many in ways he will never know. It had been thirty-six years since I had been sexually abused in Clara on that summer scouting holiday; it was so long ago and so far behind me now that I'd assumed my own painful memories had been neatly filed away somewhere in my mind. But there's a well-known truism that buried emotion and negative feelings will eventually rise to the surface. They can never stay buried while they remain active and unresolved.

My own story of sexual abuse was now rarely far from my waking thoughts and inhabited my frequent nightmares on random nights. Whenever I travelled from Galway to Dublin by rail, the train – depending on which one you took – would make its scheduled two-minute stop at the railway station in Clara. It was a part of the journey that always unsettled me. I watched through the window as the familiar grey-bricked, detached two-storey station with its three chimneys came into view, as the train slowed to a crawl and then eventually stopped at the platform. This was where my abuser was waiting to collect me when I arrived for my second visit at the start of the Easter school holidays in 1973.

Back then on that terrifying morning, there was no sign of him on the platform when I stepped off the train holding a small suitcase containing my clothes for the four-day stay. He would never have stood on the platform waiting for me. Maybe that was because he was aware that a man in a brown habit collecting a twelve-year-old boy on his own might look strange. But to anyone else in the station that morning, it would probably have seemed just natural – and that perhaps this religious brother was the young boy's uncle. But he wasn't, of course, and as I walked away from the train I wanted to tell the people on the platform that I didn't feel good about this. I wanted to tell them what he was going to do to me. I wonder how they might have reacted, these strangers watching a young boy holding a brown suitcase with a look of fear in his eyes. I'll never know.

He was waiting for me out in the car park area, away from the passengers who were coming and going.

He was a paedophile; I was his victim. Of course back then I didn't know I was a victim of sexual abuse. Such terms didn't exist in those days. All I knew was that this was our secret, to be closely guarded at all times, at the risk of being vilified – or worse – if I ever told anyone. I knew there was a river that ran through the grounds at the back of the college. What if I happened to fall in and drown accidentally? No one would know any different ...

There were nights the horrifying dreams would cause me to jump out of bed. It was as though by jumping out of bed, I was getting away from whatever else was in there with me. On those occasions, I would turn on the television and sleep in an armchair. It reached the point where I could no longer sleep in the darkness; I would leave all the lights in my apartment switched on and the radio in the kitchen playing music through the night. And it got worse.

I found myself switching channels on my car radio anytime I would hear a song that I associated in my mind with those times. I remember thinking, on the evenings when I walked along the cliffs at Renville, in Oranmore, close to where I was renting an apartment, that I couldn't live with this locked inside my head for much longer.

On a rational level I knew exactly what was going on because I had learned about it during my training in psychotherapy. What was happening deep inside me was what is known as an 'abreaction', a term used in psychoanalysis. An abreaction is the unconsciously galvanised reliving of an experience, in order to purge it of its emotional intensity. It's a type of catharsis, but usually an extremely painful and frightening experience. In short, it's the emotional discharge of unconscious material. The difficulty for many people is that such a release happens despite their best efforts to prevent it. It's almost like lifting the lid on a pressure cooker without first allowing a gentle release of some of the steam that has built up inside. This was exactly what was happening to me.

As I struggled with this internal turmoil, I realised that there was something I needed to do, something that could be put off no longer: I had to make a journey. I had to go back to Clara; I had to revisit the past. In truth, I had been thinking about this journey for quite a while, for many of the years that had elapsed since I was last in that vile place; each time I would just push it further into the back of my mind by focusing on something else. I needed to go back there for one reason: closure.

Over the months that followed I kept postponing

the trip. Considering it had been thirty-five years since I had set foot in the place, I didn't even know if St Anthony's College, run by the Franciscans, still existed. All I could remember was that it was situated on the outskirts of the town on the road to Tullamore. It wouldn't be difficult to get there, or to find the site, but still I kept putting it off, most probably out of fear. I wasn't sure why I was afraid; those events had happened a lifetime ago. But yet, each time I thought about going back, a huge sense of anxiety would rise up inside me. The fear felt so real, and the anxiety it caused made me feel like I was eleven years old again. Every time I came close to sitting into the car and setting out on the journey, I would instantly feel sick and I'd immediately postpone the plan.

In the autumn of 2008, I was offered a job in Dublin – a great opportunity to join a brand-new radio station there called 4FM, that was due to make its first broadcast in February 2009. So in November 2008, I decided I would leave Galway and return to Dublin, to take up this offer.

I still hadn't made the trip to St Anthony's College.

But then, on a Tuesday morning after an extended weekend in Dublin trying to find accommodation ahead of my move back to the capital later that month, the train stopped in Clara. A voice in my head told me to step off the train and stand on the platform. It was a calm morning, a typical autumn day with a cloudy sky and a hint of rain. The station building hadn't changed. Its chipped slate roof, red-brick chimney stacks and limestone walls all looked the same as when I'd set foot on this platform thirty-five years before. Even the sense of dread and revulsion that was firing up inside me was identical to what I had felt that morning as a twelve-year-old boy. I was right back there.

It all came back to me in an instant, more real than any dream because now I was standing in this place. I tried to recall what shoes I had been wearing – possibly sandals, or maybe runners. I remember how I'd kept my small brown suitcase by my side all the way from Heuston station; how I'd eaten the sandwiches my mother had made for me earlier that morning when I'd watched her cut them in half with the kitchen knife. All I could think of at the time was the kitchen knife, and how I wish I could take it with me. Would I really have the strength to kill him, I'd wondered.

As I stood on that platform that morning, a forty-seven-year-old man, I could feel my legs getting weak, and the beads of sweat breaking out on my forehead. I wanted to scream in an effort to get rid of whatever was still inside me. Then I heard a whistle and the sound of a horn and I looked towards the front of the train: the driver appeared to be waving at me, just as he had done all those years ago.

I quickly got back on. I sat down at the window and the train slowly moved alongside the platform as my heart pounded. I felt a knot in my stomach as I thought I saw a young boy standing on the platform holding a small brown suitcase, staring straight at me, watching the train slowly pulling away, travelling under the bridge and out of sight. The boy was me, his young life halted due to abuse. He was trapped in time, too young to know what to do because he'd made a promise he had to keep. I started to cry for him, wiping my eyes as we picked up speed.

I wanted to pull the emergency cord and stop the

train. I wanted more than anything to run back along the railway line and put my arms around him and comfort and protect him; I wanted to reassure him that the abuse was in the past now.

As the train gathered speed, I kept telling myself that there was no boy on the platform – but there was, and that November day I knew he would remain there forever until I went back and took him away from 1973 – so that he would no longer remain trapped in the guilt and shame of his terrifying ordeal. Only then would he be free to live his life far beyond the ghostly shadow of his predator, and of the pain and the anguish he had felt all his life.

I couldn't sleep that night; I couldn't bear to get into bed. I stayed up into the early hours waiting to go to work, watching Barack Obama deliver his victory speech at Grant Park in his home city of Chicago before a crowd of a quarter of a million. I still remember shivering, with a deep sense of pride, when the president-elect said, 'The road ahead will be long; our climb will be steep. We may not get there in one year, or even in one term; but America, I have never been more hopeful than I am that we will get there.'

And all through the night, the crowds kept cheering and crying out the words of his campaign slogan, 'Yes, we can! Yes, we can!'

The following day, after a long, sleepless night, I had to make final plans with my landlord to move out of the Galway apartment that weekend and pay him what he was owed. I would pack my belongings and return to Dublin the following Sunday. This was also my last week on the Galway Bay FM breakfast show, so there were a lot of loose ends to tie up before I returned to my home town.

When I came off air that morning, I made a phone call and booked an appointment to visit a well-known shaman the following day. A colleague whom I had trained with in college had recommended him, as he seemed to have a natural gift for helping to heal survivors of abuse. Having spent some years living in a community in Oklahoma, in the USA, Kevin had returned to his native County Clare shortly before his elderly mother had passed away some years earlier, and decided to stay. The west of

Ireland is steeped in spirituality, and its beautiful landscapes and wide open spaces are renowned for their healing nature. Kevin's belief was that the years we spend trying to repair our life following abuse must become a spiritual journey of self-discovery, rather than a mental and emotional wilderness filled with regrets and self-doubt.

Chapter 11

FINDING CLOSURE

Closure is so exclusively private, and it has a different meaning for each of us. Finding closure can be relatively straightforward for some, but harder to achieve for others. Closure is the act of making peace with your inner wounded child, in the case of early childhood abuse, then drawing that younger part of you towards your heart, allowing it to integrate and find its true home within the greater self. Whether after the death of a loved one, or following the end of a relationship, or hidden deep within the grief of abuse, the task of bringing closure to a life that feels as though it has been broken beyond repair is so personal, we often have to wait years to find out if it has worked, and if our grief has set us free. Sometimes it doesn't and we must carry the grief and the pain within us for the rest of our lives.

Standing on the station platform in Clara on that late autumn day in 2008 had made the memories of my abuse very present and real again. It was as though I had gone back to my past and unlocked a door I had kept firmly bolted and beyond my conscious awareness for years. As I mentioned earlier, painful memories will always find their way back to the surface, no matter how deeply they have been buried.

Ahead of my meeting with my shaman, Kevin, I had explained to him that I wanted to confront my past without confronting my abuser, who, for all I knew, could be dead. I just wanted something awful inside me to heal. I told Kevin about my train journey experience two days earlier. He commended me on being so true to myself. 'Your journey to healing has already begun. It is unstoppable now,' he explained. 'That young boy is waiting for you to come back and get him, to bring him back home for good.' I found myself becoming upset at the idea that I had left a twelve-year-old boy stranded on an old railway platform for over thirty years, but Kevin assured me that this is not how it works.

When I arrived at Kevin's place for my appointment, he told me he was going to do a 'healing touch' session. He explained that this gentle process would balance and realign my flow of energy, which had been badly disrupted – blocked, even – by the pain and anxiety my abuse had caused me all those years ago. He began the session by closing his eyes and calming his mind; in the background was the low sound of two beating drums. They beat in such a way that the sound resonated deep inside me. Kevin explained that he wanted to be fully present with me. He told me then that he was focusing the main intention on my highest good, and made a series of slow, sweeping motions above my head with a rattle he held in his hand. He told me to listen carefully to the voice of the rattle, and that I would soon experience the beginning of my healing.

Kevin then told me that it wasn't the years of blocking the experience of my abuse from my conscious awareness that had caused the anxiety, but the trauma caused at the time by the actual abuse. The healing process would eliminate blockages in my energy field so that I would be left in an optimal state for healing to occur. This centring process was similar to easing gently into a state of meditation. Finally, towards the end of my session, Kevin slowed down the pace of the rattle. The drums slowed to a single beat. After a few minutes I opened my eyes. I felt energised and fresh. The only way I can describe it is that there was a gentle strength within me, that I didn't recognise. Kevin explained that this was the strength of the ancient spirits of my ancestors that would accompany me on the journey to healing.

The two great scars that remain in the aftermath of abuse are guilt and shame. In therapy I learned that guilt is feeling bad about something you have done, while shame is feeling bad about who you are. Kevin explained that the only way to heal the trauma of the past was to permit myself to accept that I had been there through no fault of my own, and that now that world no longer existed. Memories can be healing; they can also become punishing scars if we never give them the chance to heal.

Carrying the burden of the past into the present causes such huge anxiety that we can never imagine a peaceful future. It's perfectly natural to look back and feel regret and anger, but it's equally important to replace any guilt that continues to block our journey out of the darkness with a clear conscience. I am reminded here that if we can't love ourselves, we can't expect to truly love another person. This is why many who have been sexually abused find it difficult to express their deepest feelings and love at a later stage in their lives. To accept love from someone is to leave ourselves wide open to being deceived again. To love someone is to invite abuse again. Self-forgiveness is so important because the guilt and shame you have carried for so many years often makes you feel that you were to blame for what happened to you.

To accept blame for something you were not responsible for will forever overshadow the purity and innocence of your childhood. But by forgiving yourself for believing that you were at fault, you will restore this purity and innocence to its rightful place: to where it belonged back then when you were that child. It doesn't matter how long this process takes; it will just wait until the time is right.

I have heard it said on occasion, mostly by religious fundamentalists and zealous fanatics, that we are all destined to experience different types of painful circumstances as though it has been mapped out for us by some higher religious source in order to test our faith. I recall one stranger quoting words from St Peter to me one evening many years ago after I gave a talk to a group of abuse survivors: 'these trials will prove that your faith is worth much more than gold that can be destroyed'. While I could never accept the idea that my abuse could be regarded as a test of my faith – a notion I find both warped and absolutely repulsive, as though many people are destined to be subjected to abuse so that they might learn from their experiences at some higher level, in the same way that I don't believe that multiple system atrophy was sent to me to test my faith – I now understand how much positive growth has come from slowly accepting that I am so much bigger and stronger than my abuser could ever be. Abuse can never be regarded as some outlandish test of faith, but the resilience that grows once this abuse is gently and carefully consigned to the past creates an empathy within us which allows others to see that healing is possible, and far more preferable than a life spent fearing the past. Each of us has more courage and resilience inside us than we give ourselves credit for. With each unexpected challenge that life throws at us, whether losing a job, caring for a sick child or parent, or dealing with a life-threatening illness, we build up deposits of resilience as we deal with each of these challenges. Death is out there somewhere, but I like to think it'll be a very long time before it gets near me because my resilience will see it as a challenge worth keeping at a distance.

As I drove away from Kevin's that day, I felt more relaxed than I had in a long time. I also experienced what I can only describe as feelings of being supported and guided, as if by some higher power or universal life force. With greater mental clarity than I'd experienced for a long time, I was able to make a firm commitment to myself that I would return to Clara the following Saturday, two days later.

Some months earlier, I had been looking through some old photographs my mother had carefully stored away in the attic of our family home. Perhaps it was just coincidental (although I don't believe in coincidences) that I came across an old photo taken of me around the time of my twelfth birthday, in 1973. I couldn't help thinking that I looked so sad in the picture. My smile seemed like such an effort. Of course I knew only too well why I was so sad. I slipped it into my jacket pocket. Maybe I was meant to find that exact photograph at that precise moment because I can't think of any reason why I would have chosen that one to take away with me over all the others I had looked through. I must have known deep down that I would eventually need it.

It was a damp, cold morning when I set out on the ninety-minute journey to Clara. Kevin texted me along the way to tell me he had lit a candle, and he was sending me lots of healing energy. I was grateful to him. I had no idea what I was going to find once I arrived in Clara, or what I expected to take away from the visit; all I knew was that I had to do it. The photo of my twelve-year-old self sat on the passenger seat beside me.

I had never driven into Clara as an adult; I barely remember what the town looked like. The last time I drove along these unfamiliar streets I was a scared young boy in the car of a paedophile. I found myself glancing over at the photograph on the passenger seat; at the face of the boy who must have been terrified as he looked out the window at the strangers and the names above the shop fronts, knowing what lay ahead of him.

Renee Fredrickson, in her book *Repressed Memories: A Journey to Recovery from Sexual Abuse*, talks about the power of dissociation, and how it gets you through a brutal experience, letting your basic survival skills operate unimpeded: 'Your ability to survive is enhanced as the ability to feel is diminished ... You are disconnected from the act, the perpetrator and yourself ...'

Back then I had found a way to become 'dissociated' somewhere in my head when I knew that the abuse was inevitable. It was as if I was outside of my physical body so I couldn't feel the physical pain. I was only starting to fully understand that now, as I drove through the small country town – the way the human mind can detach itself from the abuse it's being subjected to. So here I was, thirty-five years later, experiencing once again that same feeling of dissociation – as though I was being prevented from crossing a thin line for my own safety, while viewing the story of an abused boy from a distance.

Shortly after ten o'clock that Saturday morning in November 2008, after what felt like a lifetime spent trying to muster the courage and the resilience to do it, I found myself standing outside St Anthony's College – or at least what was left of it. The entrance had been secured by huge wooden padlocked gates. Beyond the gates lay a building site.

I parked my car out of sight of passing motorists, set in from the main road, and walked back to where the stylish gates had once stood. I had hurried out through them as a terrified young boy trying to make my way back to the railway station. It looked as though, to the right where there had once been acres of green fields and football pitches, two new housing estates were well under construction. To the left lay the remains of what was once the Big House and boarding school, doors and windows covered over with sheets of corrugated iron, and fencing that blocked any of the small avenues and walkways that led to and from the house.

I looked around me to make sure I wasn't attracting any unwanted attention. It was a misty morning, a light rain falling, and the streets around the town were deserted. I scaled the high gates, easing myself over the top and down the far side. For a moment, I stared around the empty grounds. I was on the inside once again. It appeared so much smaller than what I had remembered; it seemed enormous to me back then.

I took the photo out of my pocket and studied the tall, thin boy with the heartbroken smile. 'We're back,' I said out loud.

I then walked slowly towards the ruins of the old

house, where the abuse had taken place. There was no one here except me. It felt strange as I recalled how busy it had been back then. There always seemed to be buses and vans coming and going, football matches being played on the pitches, cub scouts and leaders wearing different-coloured neckerchiefs. I stood in the light misty rain, holding the photo to my chest, staring up at the circular window on the first floor. I looked around again carefully, checking to make sure I was alone.

I stood listening to the sound of birds in the distant trees and the sound of the River Brosna as it rolled along at the back of the football pitch. This was what I had been terrified to come back to, for all those years. In one sense it felt as though it had been a pointless journey, but then I realised as I looked at the photo again that I hadn't come here for me – I had come here to find something, or someone, who had been stuck here in time.

As I stood beside the house, I wondered how many other small boys had suffered in this evil place. I wondered if any of them had over the years made a journey back here like mine. I noticed a small cemetery to my left, below a sloping green hill in the shadow of a giant oak tree. I opened the rusty gate and wandered around the graves – all identically marked with small black iron crosses, each one bearing a name. I recognised a few of the names; some dead for years, others more recently passed. My abuser's name wasn't there.

The rain was getting heavier now, as if the past was being washed away in those moments. I held the photo tight against my pounding heart, imagining I was giving this poor lost boy his directions back home, assuring him that it was time for both of us to leave that pain and torment behind us – back there in 1973 where it should remain forever. I looked at the photo again, as the drops of rain splashed against its fading colours, and just for a moment I thought the boy's smile had changed. I looked up and spat at the wall of the house and walked back to my car.

That Saturday morning sits somewhere in the distant past now, as though out of the sadness and uncertainty of a difficult journey had come a new strength to help me face whatever might lie ahead, once I had silenced the demons of a partly lost childhood. That strength has served me through other challenges over the years since then, including the occasions when I have had to say goodbye to old friends who no longer share this journey with me; perhaps in spirit they watch over these words as I continue to tell this story.

When I look back on my life so far, I can see a common thread as I sit here reading these words. I realise now that no matter how difficult life became for me, I found the strength somewhere inside to keep on turning up, whether it was in the words of a song; or during a chat over tea and toast with my parents; in the belief that the spirit of my father still walks with me and has my back; in a motivational quote that I just happened to read at the precise moment I needed it; or in the reassuring voice of someone who might never know that it was their words that made me hold on tighter and aim higher. Who would have thought that I would finally meet the woman I was beginning to believe didn't exist. Well she does, thankfully. She has just made me a cup of tea. She has shown me the way, during the times I lost it and almost gave up looking. Whenever resilience weakens, she googles its definition and hands it to me to read out loud.

It might have been easier during the darkest moments to give up, but thankfully I never did. If depression has taught me one thing, it's that I am constantly being tested to my very core, as I am now on this Sunday afternoon as the last vestiges of autumn slip away outside my writing window. Perhaps all our paths are already mapped out for us in advance. If that's the case, then maybe the reason I studied ways of helping others was because I would need some of my own medicine to support me through something I never could have imagined lay ahead of me – a bit like the 'before' and the 'after'. If life can be divided into two parts, and I have just drawn a line under Part One, then Part Two is where the story becomes very challenging.

Part Two

Part Two

Chapter 12

THE DEFINITIVE DIAGNOSIS

I was admitted to hospital on a Tuesday afternoon in June 2018, six weeks after my father's funeral. My neurologist decided that results could be achieved faster by undergoing a fortnight of tests as in inpatient in a concerted effort by his medical team to establish what was going on inside me, and hopefully to arrive at a diagnosis. I had only been a hospital inpatient once in my life, fifty-one years previously when I was almost six years old. The memories I have of that time are ones of isolation and fear. I think I can even recall feeling deserted in my small world by everyone I knew. At that time, my doctor had thought it best to remove my tonsils and adenoids. I can also remember the joy of coming home, and never wanting to see mashed parsnips and carrots again.

I have no recollection of what the weather was like all those years ago in October 1966, but I can still vividly remember it was a hot summer's day in June 2018 when I stepped out of the car and stared up at what undoubtedly is a very fine if slightly menacing-looking piece of architecture. It is named after a nun called Mother Mary Vincent Whitty, born in Wexford in 1819, who was responsible for building twenty Convents of Mercy, including a Mater Hospital in Queensland. She is buried in Brisbane. I'm tempted to say, you can take the Mater out of Ireland, but you can't take the Irish out of the Mater. My two weeks of tests were taking place in the Mater University Hospital, one of Dublin's five acute-care hospitals and centres of excellence, and my brother David had taken time off work and kindly dropped me there. I had been told to enter through the Whitty Building, where the reception area looks more like that of a multinational research facility. Ground-to-ceiling windows graced the front of the building, large shrubs and a gentle waterfall took up a vast area of the ground floor, and the back walls were dotted with art work, no doubt aimed at relaxing the man who had just walked in off the street carrying an overnight bag that looked so over-packed he was clearly staying for more than one night.

I eventually sat in front of a woman tasked with gathering my information and turning me into a hospital inpatient. She appeared to be having a challenging day. Humility, I remind myself, is the best policy. You're in a hospital, and you'd really prefer if everyone in here was your friend.

I sat down and studied her form. She looked completely stressed out. She deserved respect and gratitude, so I decided to be the bearer of both. I asked her if she would like some Rich Tea biscuits for her tea break. Judging by her reaction, it was clearly a question she had never before been asked by a soon-to-be inpatient. She seemed overwhelmed by my offer as I held out the packet of biscuits to her.

The questions were standard, with just one exception: 'Religion?'

'What are the choices?' I asked.

She looked at me as she took a bite of a biscuit. 'Only you'd know that,' she replied.

'Is this in case you need to call a priest for me?' I asked, quite seriously.

She started typing. 'So, it's Roman Catholic?'

To which I replied, 'I suppose so ...'

I have always had an unresolved relationship with God. I can only speak for myself here but I've always had mixed feelings and contradictory views about who he is, and what he is – I use the term 'he' here because God has been referred to as a male for thousands of years. Do I believe in God? My answer to that question is a resounding yes. I do believe in God. I'd feel like I was missing out on something truly exciting if I believed that God was a fake. There must be a God. Otherwise little if anything of my last sixty years makes much sense. However, do I believe in a person called God? No I don't. There couldn't possibly be a single 'person' who could equate to the God-like presence that I feel around me like some kind of transpersonal power, especially when I am standing by the sea, or walking in a beautiful ancient forest.

I took the lift to the fourth floor and walked towards the double doors under the big blue 'Neurology' sign. I could see nurses and patients down along the corridor behind these locked doors. Then I heard a buzzer and a loud click. The door opened. I stepped inside and watched it close behind me. It locked again with a loud click. Hospital wards have that humbling effect, where suddenly you're stripped of status, knowledge, career ... even the cards in your wallet hold no currency in here. I started walking towards the nurses' station I'd spotted halfway along the corridor, which had a perfectly shiny floor surface, and the distinct disinfected smell of hospital.

Hospitals are a mixture of contradictions and conundrums. I've always had great difficulty trying to figure out how you can feel better when you are surrounded by people who are sick. A hospital resembles one of those far-away countries that you have no real interest in visiting during your lifetime; then you suddenly realise that you have no choice in the matter. Your plane has had to make an emergency landing in one of them, and you now have to spend time there whether you like it or not.

Usually the advance notice of your admission comes by way of a quick and courteous phone call. A bed is about to become available sometime in the afternoon. You're told to wait by the phone: you are now on official standby and another call will follow soon. You should be on your way to work, but you're not. Your routine grinds to a halt and all at once time stands still. You spend an hour packing. The bag is too big. You change everything into a smaller bag. Now there's not enough space. Then you remember this is a hospital – not a hotel in Alicante.

My mother, bless her, had dropped around a dressing gown and slippers that belonged to my father. She had also slipped the packet of Rich Tea into my bag while I was otherwise distracted.

I couldn't help wondering as I zipped the bag closed if this was how my father was feeling as he prepared to leave home for his stay in the Mater Private, adjacent to where I'd be spending my time. The phone eventually rang. It was the professor's secretary. My files had been sent across to the ward ahead of my arrival. I was told to be there by two o'clock; it was all very efficient. They were hoping that by the end of my fortnight in hospital they would have a precise picture of the problem. By now I could only second-guess what that was going to be.

Eventually, after signing some forms, and having my ID bracelet attached to my wrist, I was brought to the family room – which doubles as a waiting area if your bed space isn't quite ready – by a wonderfully chatty nurse who asked me if it was still a beautiful day 'outside'.

'Yes, it's a heatwave. Apparently it's going to last for the week.'

'Just my luck,' she replied. 'I've another five days.

That's one of the benefits of night shift: you get to lie out in the garden all day.'

I can't think of any benefit of being on a twelve-hour night shift, but this was a side of life I'd get plenty of time to witness first-hand over the coming fortnight. Her badge informed me her name was Mary – Senior Staff Nurse on the ward, essentially the boss. Polite and to the point, she had a beautiful Malaysian accent. During my time in her care, we'd end up having some great conversations about places in the world we had both been to.

I changed out of my street clothes, and within minutes had officially become an inpatient. I put on the dressing gown and slippers, and pyjama bottoms, all of which were quite at odds with what I would normally wear at home.

Just as I settled into the armchair, the door swung open. A man in a dressing gown and slippers, pyjama bottoms, stood in the doorway. 'Can I come in?' he shouted.

'Please do!' I replied. I stood up and watched him as he moved forward.

His arms and upper body looked as though they

were conducting an orchestra while he was trying to fight his way out of a straitjacket. 'I'm Mike,' he said with a huge effort. 'Have you got the remote?'

I did, and I handed it to him. 'I'm Gareth.' It didn't appear to be a good time to shake hands.

Mike, I would soon discover, had advanced Parkinson's disease, and the dyskinesia, which involves uncontrollable movement of the body's limbs and head, was deeply uncomfortable and painful to watch.

'What are you in for?' he asked, his head shaking and twitching.

'Tests,' I replied.

'What kind of tests?'

'I'm being tested for multiple system atrophy.'

The shaking stopped. 'That's a new one to me. I never heard of it. Ah well, you'll get them all in this place ... every incurable bastard of a disease ... they're all here.' He turned in gyrating movements and aimed towards the door. 'Welcome to the madhouse. You're late for lunch but you're early for tea.'

Mike Parkinson's, as he quickly became known, would become one of the many kind patients to welcome me in the first couple of days of my stay.

A hospital ward is like a transient family. For two or three days you might spend what seems like hours talking to another patient. Eventually it's like you've both become good friends, until the nurse casually mentions that he was discharged the previous day; gone without a word of goodbye. I would learn in my time in hospital, especially in a ward where cures were as rare as miracles, that no one was there to make new friends.

The majority of patients had chronic life-restricting illnesses – this is where you come, I was told on my first day by a patient in a tracksuit, when the odds are stacked against you.

'Are you a gambling man?' he asked.

I shook my head.

'Never too late to start,' he replied.

I dozed in the armchair after I had my tea. It was almost half past eight when I woke. The visitors had all gone home. Nurses from the night shift were well into their final rounds of the wards with a huge mobile bureau of medication. It looked like an old wooden music organ with its quaint, varnished lid-opened back; inside were hundreds of jars and boxes of pills and tablets. I was handed a small plastic thimble with four tablets and a similar plastic thimble filled to the brim with a gooey orange-coloured liquid that looked and smelled like car engine oil. The nurse explained I was to take this in one swallow. She then informed me, as I was trying not to gag on this revolting gloop, that it would 'help my bowel to open' before I went to sleep.

Suddenly, I felt like a helpless senile old man having his bowel movements discussed by a nurse young enough to be his daughter who looked like she'd been lying out in the sun all day. I just wanted to go home. As soon as she was gone, I lay on my side and watched the sun setting in the summer sky. I could feel myself spiralling into a black hole somewhere in my head. Is this how the rest of my life was going to be? I couldn't help thinking of all the plans I had made, and all the places I wanted to see with Paula. San Francisco, Boston, Prague, British Columbia, the Lake District in England, all seemed out of our reach until we knew what we were facing here. Now

I was wearing a dressing gown, swallowing some obnoxious lubricating sludge to prevent my intestines from forgetting what they were meant to do regularly. How long before the rest of my body decided to go out in sympathy?

Just as I could feel myself drifting off, the door swung open. Scott, a fellow patient, introduced himself. He was wearing a dressing gown that would put Joseph's technicolour dreamcoat to shame. Scott sold second-hand cars, and told me a nice Mercedes E class would suit me – an E220, preferably a convertible. It just so happened he had the very one in stock. I asked him what he was in for.

'Something's wrong with my back, but they've found nothing so far.' He shrugged. 'C'est la vie. We'll wait and see.' He rubbed his hands together, 'Now, I think it's time for a cup of tea … do you take sugar?'

'Just one, please,' I replied. 'Thanks.'

Scott left to get the tea and Tony walked in, carrying an armful of books. 'Do you read?' he asked. Setting down the books on my bedside table, he extended his hand and shook mine. He told me he'd been in now for three weeks. His daughter had brought in practically his entire book collection, and he appeared to be the self-appointed ward librarian. 'Brooksy, they call me now, like in Shawshank!' He left me with a Grisham thriller, always a good reliable, and gathered up the rest. He pulled the door behind him and the room was quiet again.

I don't remember falling asleep but I woke late into the night. The corridor lights shone through the window in my door. I noticed to my left on the nightstand a cold cup of tea and a copy of *Motoring News*. I fell asleep again and dreamed that I was sitting on the ground in the yard in Shawshank prison. Andy Dufresne was reading out a letter that we had just received from Brooks Hatlen: 'Dear fellas, I can't believe how fast things move on the outside. I saw an automobile once when I was a kid, but now they're everywhere. The world's went and got itself in a big damn hurry.'

During those long two weeks, it seemed that the world as I knew it was continuing fine out there without me. I'd thought lots of people would miss me – or maybe they were just too busy to text. In this place where time stood still, everyone was the same. Social status, property ladder, job titles, holiday homes, salary, debt, wealth – none of it mattered. No one really cared what you did for a living or where you came from. It wasn't important in the big scheme of things. The only really important questions anyone asked were, 'When can I go home?' and 'Do you have the remote?'

At the end of two weeks all the diagnostic possibilities had been exhausted and eliminated, one by one, until there was only one remaining. It was now official: I had multiple system atrophy. I often wonder about Mike, Scott, Tony and Nurse Mary. I hope Mike is leading a better quality of life following the procedure to have an apomorphine pump inserted surgically. I never got round to taking Scott's E220 convertible for a test drive, and I have yet to return that John Grisham book to Brooksy. As for Nurse Mary, I like to think she finally got the chance to visit her family at home in Malaysia. Most of all, I hope they are all still 'doing life' in the nicest possible way.

Chapter 13

LIFE AFTER HOSPITAL

In the days following my discharge from hospital I felt extremely nervous. Perhaps it was just fear of the unknown, or vulnerability, now that my diagnosis was official. There was no going back for further check-ups or tests, because there is absolutely nothing that can be done to alter the course of this illness.

Diagnosing many of the neurological diseases

we hear about today, including MSA, is done by way of a long and exhaustive process of elimination. This process begins by scientifically comparing all of the symptoms of every known neurological and autoimmune disease that can affect the human brain; then, one by one, the neurologists painstakingly eliminate the illnesses they believe you do not have. As I mentioned earlier in this book, the diagnosis of MSA can sometimes take months, often years. In my case, from start to finish – from presenting to my family doctor, being referred to a neurologist for tests, then spending two weeks in an acute-care public hospital as an inpatient – it took fifteen weeks.

I always recall that period in weeks rather than months, as there was never a single week without at least one crucial test scheduled for me – MRIs, blood tests, blood pressure monitoring, a prostate check, a bladder examination, a respiratory investigation, and so on. As those weary and worrying fifteen weeks passed slowly by, with each new test I was sent for, I would fight to find deep down within me whatever vestiges of hope remained. I would then try to focus that hope on only one outcome: that my medical team might surely find something – anything – other than MSA.

This endless list of screenings and tests is done so that the neurologists can be as certain as possible that they are giving the patient the correct diagnosis. To effectively be told that you are dying from an incurable illness and that you should go home and 'get your affairs in order', only to be later re-diagnosed and told that you do not have a terminal disease, is a scenario no one wants to even contemplate, much less ever have to experience.

As diagnostic skills continue to improve, thanks to the giant strides being made in the field of multi-dimensional magnetic resonance imaging, I expect we will begin to see a huge change in the number of people being diagnosed with greater specificity and, more importantly, much sooner than is currently the case. Since getting to know my own neurology team over the past three years, I realise that theirs is a highly complex, specialised field which carries awesome responsibilities. Those who devote their time and energy to this work should command nothing less than the utmost respect.

In the day or so following my discharge, it was almost as if I had left something important behind me in the ward. Something that was unquantifiable because it had no familiar name. Yet I felt deeply uncomfortable without it. Could it have been the hope of being diagnosed with something curable that I was still clinging to when I was admitted? Was it the way the staff all got behind me from the moment I arrived, and were willing me on to leave a fortnight later with better news than I had anticipated? Was it the patient camaraderie that comes from a shared sense of loss that only very ill people can recognise in each other? Or could it have been the sense of grief that I began to feel more and more deeply as each day passed without an answer, and another illness more preferable to MSA was eliminated?

I missed the care and attention from the staff on a ward that had become my world for two weeks of fulltime, full-on hospital living. This feeling drifted in and out during my first few days back home after Paula had returned to Cork and I was alone again. The workers at the hospital were wonderful in their ability to make you feel as though you were the only one. All through their careers, they share their hospital shifts with patients whose lives are hovering on the brink and who need to be able to find a source of hope; then, after all that, they can still find the energy and enthusiasm to share their home time with partners and children. They help with school homework, do the washing, ironing, cooking, supermarket shopping and parent-teacher meetings, while also looking in on their parents; yet where does their hope come from?

There is an unconscious sense of reassurance that comes from being looked after night and day by highly trained people who will do whatever they can to make you feel better, even though it's the last place you want to be. Of course you would prefer to be at home, but they do their best to give you a temporary home, somewhere that you quickly settle in to. You get to know their voices, even from a distance. Your name rolls off their tongue as if they have known you personally for years. With each new test they carry out, there is renewed hope that maybe this is going to be the one that will help solve the mystery of your symptoms and then point to the cure for the underlying problem.

Now that I had been discharged, I knew that any hope of the neurologists finding a cure was behind me.

There was also a strange feeling of elation as I turned the key in the door of my apartment: at least now I knew what my diagnosis was. It had a name. The months of worrying might have brought me to this point, but now at least there was no need to worry anymore about what it might or might not be. There would be no need for any more humiliating and painful invasive testing; no more worrying each morning about what part of my anatomy was going to be the focus of the consultant's attention that day.

The discomfort I had felt on leaving hospital lifted within the first twenty-four hours, and it was replaced by a strange peace of mind; strange because there was no good news in what I had been told two days earlier. I hadn't arrived back home with a clean bill of health. There was nothing to celebrate, other than that the hospital was at last behind me. I wouldn't have to go through that ordeal again. At least I hoped I wouldn't. Yet whatever lay ahead of me now was nothing short of terrifying.

The finality of being discharged from hospital was matched almost by the sense of finality that had come with the diagnosis the previous day. It was a Saturday morning; the ward felt empty. Many of the inpatients had gone home for the weekend. Those who couldn't, for whatever reason, were resting in their rooms. An intern neurologist was on call in case of emergency (while she was also expected to deal with the madness of the busiest A & E in the country over an entire weekend).

Otherwise, the ward was eerily quiet. There was no, 'We are all delighted for you', or, 'We'll see you back here next month for some more treatment', or, 'We'll start you immediately on a new drug that has had some promising results with these types of illnesses'. Perhaps it was a sense of sadness and frustration that was hanging over the nurses' station that morning, that there was nothing else that could medically be done for me to make me better.

As I thanked them for looking after me so well, the neurologist and the two nurses on duty smiled and nodded their heads. I walked slowly – like I'd done on so many late nights and early mornings – the full length of the long corridor, my trainers squeaking on the polished, sterilised floor that I recalled also from the afternoon two weeks before when the doors had clicked shut behind me. As the automatic doors swung closed that morning, I was at last on the outside.

That evening Paula and I joined some friends for drinks and food in Canal Bar, along the banks of the Royal Canal, one of our favourite haunts whenever we shared time together in Dublin. Everyone was in great form, delighted that I was home; happy to see us both together again. But I just couldn't settle. I couldn't blend in with the good humour and enjoy the warmth that I would always feel among these kind people in what would normally be a very relaxed atmosphere. The elation I had felt during the homecoming earlier that day was quickly dissipating, and taking its place was a black, empty void that was intent on sucking me inside.

I excused myself from the company for a few

minutes that evening and went to the bathroom. I remember looking at my hands as I washed them under the running water; then I looked at my face in the mirror above the sink. Staring back at me was someone who had been told less than a day earlier that he was terminally ill. I wondered at that moment what it would feel like to be on the outside looking in, looking at this man who appeared to be perfectly well and healthy, except he wasn't. There was no hope for him, this poor unfortunate bastard. This disease was cruelly destroying his central nervous system, intent on killing him slowly. And it would. One thing I could never say to him was, 'You'll be grand' – because he wouldn't be 'grand'.

The following day Paula returned home to Cork. Normally on a Sunday I would finish my morning radio show at 11 a.m., and spend the rest of the day relaxing. If Paula was in Dublin with me for the weekend, we would often head into the city for a walk around some of our favourite shops and haunts, have a few drinks, and then come back home for dinner. That Sunday, however, she had to leave Dublin early.

It was the first time in over two weeks that I found

myself completely alone. I felt uneasy at first, and then it gradually became nothing less than terrifying. I sat in an armchair for what seemed like hours, with my hand under my chin, contemplating all I had been through over the previous fortnight. I tried to draw on my training as a therapist by telling myself that the feeling would lift; that the fear I was experiencing was caused by nothing more than what I was choosing to think about. But how could I stop it? I couldn't just stop thinking about this illness, and what it was doing deep inside me. Incurable, progressive, fatal: the three words I couldn't get out of my head.

It felt as though I had been removed for a short period from a life that I had for the most part loved and been familiar with for as long as I could remember – and now I was being reintroduced to that life, but on different terms and conditions. The landscape felt somehow different, even though nothing about it had changed.

I was still wearing the plastic identity band that a nurse had secured around my wrist on my first afternoon in hospital. It smelt of hospital. The smell instantly transported me back to a moment on the ward when I was sitting on my bed, staring out the window at the spectacle of a once-normal life I no longer was interested in being a part of.

Now I stared out at the beautiful June sunshine and the busy street below my apartment. People were out strolling, jogging, wheeling buggies, walking dogs, and generally lapping up the relaxing warmth of the summer heatwave. I was a spectator somewhere on the outside of a life that I didn't recognise anymore.

I couldn't feel how I wanted to feel. I wanted to appreciate the beautiful weather; I wanted to enjoy the music that was playing on my kitchen radio. I have always believed that music sounds so much better when the sun is shining, when you can look up at those intensely blue skies that seem to extend to infinity and continue forever in every direction. This is why summer has always been my favourite time to be on the radio playing the songs I love.

People feel better when the sun is shining. So why could I not find it in me that afternoon to feel better? Was it because I was dying? I had just been told I had a progressively fatal illness but I didn't feel like I was dying. I reminded myself that everyone dies eventually. Death is unavoidable. As Terry Pratchett once said, 'Death's not a bad guy; he's just really good at his job.'

The fact is we are all destined to die: 'No one gets out of here alive'. It's one of life's givens. So what's all the fuss about?

The truth stands that each of us harbours a deep hope that we will live healthily to a ripe old age, and when our time comes we will die painlessly, with dignity, surrounded by our loved ones who will mourn us and recall cherished memories. In an ideal world, death is supposed to come at the end of a long, happy and prosperous life; or that's the belief we like to persuade ourselves of. But our world is far from ideal and death is ultimately the end of everything we know and recognise and call our own; of all the different shades of ourselves that make up who we are and what we have come to mean to other people. It's too difficult to think about. So we don't – or at least we try our best not to. It's too dark to dwell on, and it overshadows the hope we cling to that there are certain things we should be entitled to look forward to and enjoy in years to come.

Most of us live our lives as though we're never going to die. We embrace it in such a way that we pay no attention that eventually our time will run out. We think that death is something that happens to other people, but 'not to me'. Is that not the way we should live? I would say yes, it is the only way to live. Very few people in the prime of their lives, with good jobs, money at their disposal, a happy family life, and little if any health concerns, are even remotely interested in considering the fact that some day they will die, never mind discussing it. Dwelling on death is a sign of depression, a psychiatrist told me years ago. I agreed with him back then, but I would now disagree with him. That frame of mind of not thinking about our own death changes drastically when you're told that you are dying and nothing you try to do will change that, and when you know exactly what it is that is ultimately going to cause your death.

The author Nuala O'Faolain brought Ireland to a standstill in 2008 with a radio interview she gave to her great friend and broadcaster, the late Marian Finucane. Nuala was dying. Only six weeks before recording the interview she had been diagnosed with cancer. She had inoperable tumours in her liver, lungs and brain. She was given the news quite casually by a doctor, who was about to walk past her while she was sitting in the corridor of her local emergency department in New York where she lived. She stopped the doctor and asked him if he had received any results back from tests she had undergone earlier that day. She was then told by him in an offhand way that she had cancer and that it was incurable. Nuala told Marian that she was devastated – not just by the results, but by the way she had been told. She refused the offer of chemotherapy and explained that she decided the following day to come back home to Ireland to die.

The interview made for difficult listening. O'Faolain's brutal honesty and her absolute refusal to accept chemotherapy and to 'battle to the bitter end' was something Irish people were certainly not used to hearing. We are not accustomed to such openness, especially from someone so many listeners felt they knew in some way, from her own radio work down through the years and her bestselling memoir, *Are You Somebody?* For a lot of people, there was something deeply shocking in hearing Nuala speak so honestly and unreservedly about death that day.

Nuala O'Faolain's interview is still regarded by many as one of Irish radio's most poignant and memorable moments; some consider it to be the finest interview ever. I'm sure there have been plenty of radio debates and discussions about death, but I can't recall any of them in the same way that I remember this heartbroken yet rebellious woman shrugging off the pieties and taboos that surround mortality, when she was so close to her own impending death.

We are renowned here in Ireland for the way we deal with those who die – in celebrating their lives and giving them 'a good send-off' – but we're hopeless when it comes to coping with those who are in the act of dying. In fact, many of us choose to simply run and hide. The words that I most recall from Nuala O'Faolain's interview are these: '... I think there's a wonderful rule of life that means that we do not consider our own mortality. I know we seem to, and to remember, "Man, thou art but dust", but I don't believe we do. I believe there's an absolute difference between knowing you are likely to die, let's say within the next year, and not knowing when you are going to die – an absolute difference.'

For me this made perfect sense. It was far from comfortable, but in hindsight it served as a useful lesson for me in learning to discern what is truly important and sustainable in this precious, fragile life; and, more important still, to recognise what is simply a waste of valuable energy and priceless time.

I called my programme director at Classic Hits that Sunday afternoon to let him know that I would not be back in work until Tuesday. I knew I needed another full day to get over the hospital experience, and to get used to wearing normal clothes again. So, after a couple of hours in the armchair, I thought it might be a good idea to get out into the sunshine and get some fresh air.

As I pulled on a light jacket, aware the temperature outside was in the mid-twenties, I glanced across at the large carrier bag packed with medication that sat on my dining room table. Before leaving hospital the previous day, I had been given a long and illegible prescription, based on the findings of the various tests that had been conducted. I dropped it into my local pharmacy shortly after arriving home. I still hadn't unpacked the bag twenty-four hours later.

There were pills to help me sleep, while there were others to relax my muscles and prevent 'restless legs syndrome' – which is an uncontrollable urge to move your legs in bed at night, caused by tingling, crawling and pulling sensations in the calf muscles. It feels like you're being stung by nettles on the lower backs of your legs while lying on your side. There were pills to prevent REM sleep behaviour disorder (RBD), which can cause someone with MSA to physically act out dreams that most other people just silently sleep through. If for example during a nightmare you imagine that you are being chased by a wild bull, eventually you will just wake up gasping, maybe perspiring, with your heart pounding. Someone with RBD however will start roaring and cursing out loud at the animal, their arms will be flailing in the bed; they might even lash out with their fists in order to protect themselves from being gored, or end up falling out of the bed; and all of this while they are still asleep. The very real danger is that you will cause yourself an injury or, worse, that you will injure your partner lying beside you during one of these frightening dream experiences.

There were also pills to ease bladder issues and bowel problems; tablets to regulate blood pressure; drugs to counteract myoclonus (frequent quick, involuntary muscle jerks that shoot up through your body like minute electric shocks when you are lying in bed trying to relax), and the nightly tremors that can keep your hands and fingers twitching while you're doing your best to get a good night's sleep. I rarely experience the myoclonic shocks these days, thanks to the meds I take before bed. On top of the prescription meds, there were over-the-counter mouth sprays, nasal sprays, eye drops, painkillers, and creams for neck and muscle cramps.

This huge bag of pharma's finest had set me back well over a hundred euro – and that was just my first month's supply. I suspected that at this rate my bank account too would soon be receiving a terminal diagnosis! For someone who disliked taking even a couple of paracetamol for a headache, I was now a born-again junkie, a modern-day pharma prodigy.

Chapter 14

THE HOLIDAY THAT SHOULD
NEVER HAVE HAPPENED

A few weeks after I received my diagnosis, Paula and I decided to go to Austria for a few days. We both needed a break, preferably far away from the confusion of all that was going on at home. I made arrangements for us to travel to the stunningly beautiful town of Lermoos in the Tyrol region of the Austrian Alps. I felt that the time away together would help us to come to terms with the shock of what we had been through in the previous weeks and months, particularly the body blow of learning that I had MSA. It would also give us the chance to rekindle the bond we'd always had that is so important to us. We spent four days in the most spectacular scenery imaginable, staying at the beautiful guesthouse of our friend, Erika Mott.

I really believed that the space, beauty and peaceful solitude of that place would in some way restore a sense of normality to my life. Only in hindsight would I realise that the plan to spend a few days away together on holiday was my way of trying to bypass the awfulness of what had happened. But it wasn't that it *had* happened – it was still happening, and there was no way of bypassing that. Rather than offering an escape from everything, our time away together brought home to me, more starkly than ever, the new reality we were facing into.

The weather in Austria was beautiful that summer, much like in Ireland, where the heatwave was ongoing – but for that reason alone, it was definitely not the right place for us to have gone to under the circumstances. As I mentioned earlier, one of the many troublesome symptoms of MSA is that the internal system for regulating your body temperature no longer works properly. Although for many months – even before my diagnosis – I had been suffering night sweats in cold weather, along with an inability to sweat when the temperatures were high, in the excitement of planning our trip I had somehow forgotten this. In Lermoos, I found it impossible to deal with the soaring temperatures. I felt most days that I was descending into some form of meltdown because I couldn't perspire normally to keep my body cooled. Whenever I was outdoors, the inferno I felt inside caused my entire body to tremble. These spasms were so unbearable that on one occasion, I remember standing under a lukewarm shower in the bathroom and slowly turning the thermostat down to freezing cold. It was the only way to stop the shaking. During these times the sensation of every cell in my body being in helpless overdrive was so overwhelming that I felt like throwing up or passing out. Often I would simply lie on the floor and wait for the day to cool down and these minute vibrations to stop. Eventually I would fall asleep from the exhaustion. Meanwhile I could tell that Paula was trying to put on a brave face throughout this awful experience. I felt worse because my condition was ruining her holiday. I tried as often as I could to push myself in an effort to convince her that I really was having a wonderful time, but it was so easy for her to see through the charade. We took the cable car to the Grubigstein each day, and sat together for hours in awe of the most wonderful views from the top of the Alps across five European countries. Being at such a high altitude seemed to ease the symptoms. Perhaps this was caused by the low temperature on top of the Grubigstein. But as soon as the cable car would bring us back down the mountainside, the temperature would rise and I would feel ill again. Paula would frequently ask me to explain to her how I was feeling, whereas I found it easier just to remain silent. Even speaking during those spasms became something that caused pain and nausea. It felt better to say nothing, even though this upset her greatly at times. It was only when I explained it to her, that I wasn't purposely ignoring her or being rude, that she came to understand yet another horrible aspect of this illness.

By the time we arrived back in my apartment in Dublin, I felt like I was losing my mind. The morning after we got back, I told Paula I wanted her to go home. At first it seemed as though she hadn't heard me right, and when she didn't react, I asked her again to leave. I wanted silence. I needed to be alone. I couldn't deal with any sort of conversation or activity. It was as though I was going crazy and I didn't want her to be there when it happened. I wasn't sure what was going to happen next. I just wanted empty space. That would give me a sense of control, or so I thought. She then became deeply upset and started to pack her bags, while all I could do was sit there and wait for her to go. Down on the street outside, I watched as her car drove away. Then I came back upstairs. I had absolutely no idea what I was doing or what was happening in my life. Everything had shifted. Nothing made any sense to me anymore.

Here I was, after spending four days in one of the most beautiful places on earth with one of the kindest, most caring and loving people in the world – and I had just asked her to leave. Later that day I phoned Paula and asked her to forgive me. I said that I could only hope that maybe she could understand what was going on in my mind, because I certainly couldn't.

For weeks after my diagnosis, maybe even months, because I lost count, I constantly dwelled on the notion of a world without me in it, and how that might feel for the people I love who I'd left behind. I tried to imagine how Paula would cope with my death, and her two wonderful children, Emma and David, whose lives I had become a huge part of, and my daughters, Kerri, Katie and Aibhín. What type of world would that be? Would I have any idea of what was happening to them all, and to my old familiar world, after my death? Would I be watching from some balcony somewhere, or would I have become this invisible spirit that no one can see, but yet I'm there trying to stop the tears, trying to physically reassure my loved ones that they should move on with their lives? Or would I be furious as I watched all this, angry and bitter that this illness had terminated my wonderful life and left me alone in some astral sphere where – I was once told by a medium – all spirits find the afterlife peace that they were robbed of during their paths to death? I hated that notion, because I wanted to be beside Paula. I wanted to be able to continue writing books, even if I had to use some form of recording device because my independence was being robbed from me.

I was wrestling with death anxiety, fear of nonexistence. It's a common enough emotion, if 'emotion' is the most appropriate way to describe it – how we react to the news that we have an illness and we are never going to recover from it. We have been told we are dying and nothing can prevent it. Such terrifying words initially suffocate the life force. It seems as though the will to live is being told it's wasting its time. Is there such a thing called nonexistence? It's not even a state of mind, or a place; it's basically the ultimate form of nothingness. This is death anxiety at its most terrifying – the idea that a life so worthwhile, so loved and so well-lived can just cease to exist.

For me, death anxiety is a state of mind that throws up many feelings: fear of what lies beyond death's door, sadness that I might not be around to witness my children marry, my granddaughters graduate from college. Would my wife find someone new who might love her and ease her broken heart? Would I want her to meet someone new? I would never want to deprive someone I love of finding unexpected happiness and support in the midst of grief and loneliness.

But it's not just that. It's the absence of the physiological structure of who I am right now. I rather like my person. Like so many others, I've struggled with life. I'm almost sixty. I still have so much living to do, so many books to read, some more to write. Whenever I think of the great masters who have spent their lives making the quality of the lives of others so much better – people like Leonardo da Vinci, Mozart and Beethoven, Freud and Jung, Jesus Christ – have all of these lives vanished into nothingness, or nonexistence, despite the legacies they have left us?

My body will be sealed in a coffin and buried in the earth for the rest of time. My physical remains will return to nature. I envy those with a strong faith who believe that their souls will be reunited with their bodies on the occasion of the second coming of Jesus Christ. I have a strong faith, but it doesn't stretch that far. It's important here that I make it quite clear that I respect the beliefs and the religious practices of others. I would never call another person's faith nonsense, or a waste of time. Praying and believing in a higher power can never be a waste of time.

I told broadcaster Ryan Tubridy in an interview in August 2018 on his RTÉ Radio 1 show that I wasn't afraid of dying; I just wasn't ready to die. Ryan had invited me onto the show to discuss my recent diagnosis, my decision to leave radio, and to chat about my future plans. He also asked me about death. I think most listeners interpreted my words to mean that I had too much living still to do before I die. While that is true, what I really meant was that I have yet to make friends with death. I have yet to make a place for it in my life, so that life can co-exist alongside death.

How do you possibly even want to make friends with death, and what purpose would such a friendship serve? Ultimately the final event-moment of your entire existence and everything you ever represented and will be remembered for, will be a slow exhalation of breath and then a permanent eternal stillness, beyond which you can no longer exist as everyone knows you.

Such is death anxiety. It's almost similar to a form of grieving, even though you are not mourning a dead loved one; you are already mourning the self-realisation that you are edging closer and closer to your own death. Death anxiety is something that only human beings experience, because we are the only living beings who experience consciousness.

The only way to continue to live a happy and fulfilling life, even when you have been told no one knows how long you have left, is to accept that death is as much a part of life as love is. If we turn our backs on the part that death plays in our lives, then we compromise our ability to live fully. If we spend what's left of our time here worrying about all the time we are not going to be here, then we will have cheated ourselves out of the only opportunity we have to claim back whatever is left of our lives, and live and embrace that to the full.

First of all, it's crucial to remind myself that no one

– no one – knows what the future holds. Can I see myself out there in the future? Yes I can. Therefore I have a purpose and a place in time that has yet to unfold itself, a time that hasn't yet been created. If I can project my identity, let's call it 'the self', into the future, then I have hope within me. How do I identify my 'sense of self'? Well, for this, I have to look back at my past. I can instantly recall memories and how I overcame challenges that made me feel suicidal. Somehow I managed to see my identity, the 'self', stretching out into the future, and by doing so I was building up the resilience I needed to keep going, to follow that projection I had in my mind a picture of seeing my identity ahead of me in time to come. This helped me to overcome the feelings of nothingness and despair that I spoke about in *A Day Called Hope*. The sense of self also depends largely on memory. We grade ourselves on how we performed in the past. I'm still here, so therefore I was able to see my 'self' in the future, which is right now.

To see the world as it really is, is both devastating and terrifying. It makes routine activity almost impossible. Thankfully that day, as would occasionally happen again, Paula was ahead of me. She was able to understand why I had acted as I did, in sending her away; she was able to forgive me, because she could accept that all this was just part of a huge transition that I was being forced to go through.

Chapter 15

THE END OF AN ERA

When you love your job, you never really give much thought to the likelihood that it will have to end at some point; or to the possibility that a day might come when something beyond your control will unexpectedly end it for you.

It was a warm Friday afternoon, the last day of August 2018, when I presented my final radio show. It's a day I will never forget. The summer was drawing to a close, and so was my involvement in the world of radio I had loved being a part of for almost forty years.

The weeks leading up to that point had been difficult in the extreme. After my discharge from hospital in June, my bosses at Classic Hits wanted me back on air as soon as possible. I was drawing the biggest audience of the day with my afternoon show, and this was reflected in the substantial amount of revenue that the radio station was bringing in as a result of advertising and sponsorship deals linked directly to the show. The weeks following my return were very difficult health-wise, however, and I had to call in sick on a number of occasions, due to blood pressure problems, heavy colds and respiratory infections, as well as a depression that had taken hold at a level so deep within me that I had seriously thought about taking my own life on more than one occasion.

Even though I knew I needed to leave the radio station, I couldn't find the strength to make the decision. I was self-employed. I had virtually no savings, and I was very much aware that the state's invalidity pension wasn't going to get me very far. I also knew that the small amount I currently had in my bank account would barely get me to the end of October. It looked as though I had no choice but to continue to work.

To my listeners, my workload most likely didn't sound as heavy as it was. I presented a five-hour show each day, Monday to Friday, and a three-hour show every Sunday morning. The option was there to pre-record the weekend show, but I always chose to do it live. I guess I liked the old-style way of doing my show: if I was meant to be on air, then I wanted to actually be there! Radio presentation came easily to me, perhaps from decades of practice until I got it right; or maybe it was also because I loved what I was doing that I made it look so easy.

It was clear, however, that the stress I was feeling due to the long hours I worked and the pressure behind the scenes of a high-profile radio show would probably only speed up the decline in my health. I had a hunch that the illness was progressing faster than it should have been, and that this was all down to my rising stress and anxiety levels. In hindsight, I can see the extent to which, in the immediate period after my diagnosis, I experienced a rapid decline in my physical and mental state. At the time I couldn't distinguish whether this was because of the shock of the diagnosis, or whether the illness itself was in freefall, a state of steep decline which would be typical of the disease. My legs started to weaken more, so my walking became precarious. My balance was unpredictable because my blood pressure was out of control: one minute I was standing perfectly straight; the next I had to reach for anything close-by to hold onto to prevent me from falling over.

I still have no idea if the rapid deterioration that summer was caused by fear, and the anxiety that I no longer felt in control, or if it really was the disease that was making me feel more edgy and unnerved. I have often wondered what my life would be like now if I hadn't made an appointment to see the doctor that morning in February 2018 and was none the wiser about this illness. It's hard to believe, but the reason I was reluctant to visit him was because I would save sixty euro by not going. Money was scarce then, but looking back, it was probably the best sixty euro I'd ever spent. Many people tell me they would prefer not to be told by their doctor if they had a life-threatening illness. But I wanted to know. And so I found out.

Now I had a very serious decision to make: either I leave the job and try to survive on whatever money I had, or I stick with the high-pressure routine and watch this disease quickly consume my entire nervous system and kill me. As it turned out, the decision was unexpectedly made for me.

I was sitting in my local one afternoon having a pint, completely depressed and feeling more worthless than I had ever felt, when my phone rang. It was a good friend I hadn't spoken to since the previous Christmas. He sounded very serious, so I suspected there was some very grave news concerning his health about to come down the line.

'Gareth, how are you?' he asked pointedly.

'Not great,' I replied.

'I haven't heard you on the radio over the past few weeks. Have you left the job?'

'No. I just haven't been feeling well. In fact, I feel awful.'

'And why haven't you left?' he asked.

'I haven't left because I have no money. I need to

keep working to be able to pay bills and keep my head above water.'

'Gareth, your priority is your health, not your job. Your job will still be there in months and years to come, except you won't be doing it because you didn't heed the warning signs. You'll be long buried, and someone else will have made your old show into their own very successful show. Nothing is more important than maintaining your physical independence and your mental wellbeing. Staying in a job that is causing you enormous anxiety and stress is not going to benefit you in the long term,' he said quite abruptly. 'It will most likely kill you.'

'I'm sorry?'

'You must give yourself a chance to start living properly. That must be your priority from now on.'

There were no words. I just didn't know how to reply. It was exactly what I needed to hear. I suddenly realised that deep down, I had been hoping that someone, anyone, might turn around and tell me to stop. I desperately needed to hear someone say, 'Give yourself a chance, man! It's not worth it. You're going to kill yourself if you keep doing this. Get out and start living.' It was a moment when everything suddenly made sense. It took this kind, considerate friend, whom I hadn't seen or talked to for months, to bring me to my senses.

Next he slowly, almost methodically, spelled out something I will never forget; something I will forever be thankful for. 'You are one of my best friends. You are my priority here. You come first. You have a very serious illness that is only going to get worse – you don't need me to tell you that anymore, because you already know. You have one serious battle on your hands and you're only going to complicate the battle by trying to do too much for other people, rather than spending that time doing what you need to do for yourself. Take control here. If you don't, everything will be lost and you'll get a nice write-up in the newspapers, a few mentions on the radio news bulletins, and then you'll be history. Is that all it's really worth?'

His words were so perfectly chosen, they froze me on the spot. No reply was needed. I knew he was right in everything he said. It was my time to go. Let someone else take over the show. I needed to start planning how to live my life my way from now on, and I needed to do that immediately. I wanted to live; but more importantly, I wanted to stay alive for as long as I could.

After a few seconds of silence, he continued. 'We've been friends for more years than I can remember. I've gone to too many funerals. I certainly don't want to be going to yours for a very long time to come. I want you to leave the job behind you as soon as you can. I do not want your listeners hearing you slowly fall apart live on the radio. That's just not fair. This disease is bad enough without letting that happen. You are worth so much more than that.'

He paused again. 'I am always here for you if you need me. I trust you will give what I have said some serious consideration. Gareth, you don't know how long you have left; none of us knows how long we have left. That time, however long or short it might be, is yours and no one else's. I have yet to meet a man who's been given a second chance at life tell me he's sorry he didn't spend longer working in the office. Take care for now.'

I listened as the phone clicked and the line went

dead. I felt the urge to call him back and ask him if that conversation had really happened or if I was just imagining it. A second chance; those were his exact words. Maybe that's how I should be looking at this, instead of seeing it as an end to a career, and the start of the end of my life; maybe I should be thankful for being given a wake-up call and see this as my one chance to do something monumental – namely live more fully than I have ever lived before.

Later that afternoon I fell into a deep sleep. A couple of hours later, I woke from the horrors of a nightmare where I was about to be hit by a train – perhaps the sound of an evening train passing on the railway line close to my apartment had somehow become entangled with whatever I had been dreaming about. The pillow and the bed linen were soaked in sweat and I felt like I had a raging fever. My room was like a sauna. There seemed to be no escaping this heatwave. It was as though my brain was going into meltdown.

I slowly made my way into my small sitting room and sat in the armchair as I listened to the evening commuter traffic on the street below. I thought back over the conversation I'd had with my old friend earlier.

A few hours ago, it had seemed like the perfect solution: to wind up my career and concentrate more on living fully. But what does 'living fully' really mean? My radio career was my life – and had been for almost forty years. It was all I knew and all I ever really wanted to do. Yes, I had tried my hand at one or two other occupations and hobbies but my bedrock had always been the radio. What would I do without it? Would I just sit here in this armchair day after day? I tried to think of other ways I could pass the time – but I couldn't. Now I could feel myself starting to panic.

I had been so fortunate to have a job I loved, that I had never entertained the notion that I would someday retire from it. Presenting a radio show is one of those jobs that you can continue to do for as long as your listenership remains strong and your voice stays intact. So, what would I do with my time once I had left my work behind? What would make my life worth living now that I'd been diagnosed with an incurable illness that would eventually kill me? What was I meant to think about and how could I make plans, knowing this disease was slowly taking me apart?

I stood up and kicked the armchair. I was angry and I couldn't get rid of that feeling. Why had I been given this life-threatening sentence, when I had just found a personal happiness that I never thought I would experience? I was in the throes of the most wonderful relationship with a woman I met quite by chance, who had given my life a sense of rich beauty and belonging that I could never have imagined possible. I had a career that could still compete with the best of them. At last everything seemed to be going right for me – but now it was all going wrong. Why now? I sat down and closed my eyes, trying to think back over the words of my friend during that unexpected phone call earlier.

Now the light was fading outside my window; I must have dozed off again. As the room grew darker, my tired, scattered mind started to toy again with the idea of suicide. Fifty-seven years old and I felt like I no longer knew who I was. It felt as though I had been taken over by an invisible, destructive force and I had no control. I could hear my friend from earlier on in the day telling me to take control of my life. I was losing my body, once so alive and strong, a body that would never be the same again. I was fighting a battle that I had no hope of winning. What sort of efforts would be expected of me in the future to help to support my body against this illness – an illness that would eventually render my brain incapable of caring for me physically? Even though my mind would remain sharp and responsive, I would lose the battle to save my central nervous system; it would take a hammering. I watched the reddening sky turn darker, and began to dwell seriously on the notion that life was becoming too difficult to deal with.

I knew one of my kitchen presses was now full to the brim with prescription medication. If I mixed the antidepressants with the benzodiazepines, and threw in a couple of painkillers, I would be dead by the time it got bright outside – it would all be over. I would no longer have to put up with the relentless fear of what my life would become once this illness really started to take me down.

I have always been an outspoken advocate when it comes to trying to persuade those who are suicidal to hold onto the life that they feel they can no longer tolerate – that there is always a reason to live. An abiding memory of my morning in court in relation to my financial problems in November 2013 still sends shivers down my spine whenever I am reminded of the occasion – if I pass the Four Courts building in Dublin, or when I accidentally find some correspondence connected to my case. As I waited for my case to be called, I listened with interest as the clerk of the court called the initials of those whose cases were due to be heard before mine. On a number of occasions there was silence in the courtroom as the master of the High Court waited for a defendant to answer to his or her name being called. A barrister would inform the judge that 'the reason for my client's absence is because he [or she] passed away recently'. Each time the judge asked about the circumstances of death, the barrister would reply: 'Suicide.' All of the cases that morning involved strangers I had never heard of, who owed money to banks and other financial institutions. Most of them were men. I'm sure many of these men had families, wives, maybe young children. Their barristers were in court to tell the judge that they had taken their own life, most likely as a result of the unbearable anxiety and fear they were experiencing because they were afraid of losing their family homes due to the threats being made against them by the banks. I had considered suicide on more than one occasion when my debts became so great that only death would take away the pain of the non-stop worrying, the threats, the phone calls, the registered letters, and the never-ending nightmares that scorched my mind so badly every hour of every night I begged the darkness to let me sleep.

I often wonder about those names, those men, all these years later. I wonder if they had held on, would their lives be better today. I wonder if their young children even remember them or if their wives have remarried. I wonder if the faceless employees in suits who threatened them to the point where suicide was preferable to the notion of homelessness and disgrace in the local community ever think about them, about the positions they held in these financial institutions which required them to go after those who owed them money, to chase them down and corner them into submission. I doubt it.

For many years, I have believed that if I can just step away from the thoughts that have taken hold of my mind and are convincing me that death will stop my invisible pain, that if I can dissociate myself from my faulty thinking and imagine I am watching a conversation going on between two versions of me – the person who wants to die, and the person who beneath it all still wants to find a reason to live – then I will discover the importance of life and why it is still worth holding onto.

No one wants to suffer the invisible pain of mental anguish and the hopelessness that clouds and obscures life; but, in many people, depression is a treatable illness, and surely it's worth at least giving recovery a chance, and others the opportunity to help.

In *A Day Called Hope*, I wrote a lot about suicide. It was written mostly from my own perspective on why someone decides they can no longer continue. This is from the chapter 'Breaking the Taboo'. I really believe it is worth reading again, maybe even more than once:

'Suicide is the ultimate act of will in a faulty and warped process of self-vindication. No one can accuse me of any wrongdoing to anyone else, runs the argument in the intending suicide's mind, because I have decided to do it all by myself. I have only myself to blame. It is my own free will that has decided on this course of action. It represents freedom from a dark, windowless cell of sadness, anger, self-loathing and the sense of worthlessness. Suicide sprouts wings when nothing else – absolutely nothing that ever held importance and had a sense of hopeful structure – makes any sense. At that terrible moment suicide seems to have more going for it, in the eyes of its victims, than the nothingness of hopelessness and the prospect of an eternity of invisible pain and suffering.'

It's eighteen years since the publication of that book, and I find it so much easier to talk openly these days about my infrequent periods of depression. It still comes, often when I least expect it to. Darkness is probably a more accurate word to describe how I feel during these bleak times. It's as though I lose sight of any real purpose in my life, just like I did in a big way after I was diagnosed with multiple system atrophy in 2018. For a long time after my diagnosis, I felt robbed of that purpose; until I really started questioning myself about what exactly that purpose was. Was it my radio career? For most of my life it certainly felt that way. But that ended almost three years ago, and yet I still believe that my life has a purpose. So what is it?

Of course I love my life; I certainly don't want to die, not for a very long time, but I do believe you can continue to love the life you have but lose your sense of purpose. I have only begun to realise in recent times that behind every genuine purpose lies an even greater purpose. Sometimes you have to be patient in order to find out what exactly that is, and what it requires you to do.

I used to think that people became suicidal because they had lost their sense of purpose. Now I see things differently. The greatest purpose we can ever set ourselves is to experience life to its fullest, so there's no such thing as not having a purpose. However, one thing we cannot survive without is a deep sense of belonging – whether that's to our partner, our children, our grandchildren, our pet, to a greater power (what many people call God), or to our purpose. Some people set themselves the most arduous physical challenges, upping their game year after year with even more challenging tasks, pushing themselves harder and testing their endurance to its limits. For many of them, overcoming these challenges becomes their main purpose in life.

My purpose in life now, and by far my greatest challenge so far, is to take on this illness and beat it. Can I do this? No one diagnosed with this illness has ever beaten it, according to the clinical research and prognostic statistics that continuously remind me that it is 1) unstoppable, 2) incurable, and 3) progressively fatal. Perhaps I won't beat it, but while my purpose is to stay healthy and retain my quality of life, I won't ever give up trying.

It would have been so easy for me to give up three years ago. If I had, my condition would have deteriorated more rapidly and I would be in a far more depressing place in my life right now. That's if I was still alive. If I have learned anything from my experience as a therapist, and from my own personal experience of dealing with this awful illness, it's this: there are three things that will make you sicker than you already are: pessimism and negativity, and not taking complete control of your own healing and recovery.

As I mentioned, many of those who spoke to me during my time as a therapist yearned to have their old lives back. All they wanted was to be back there somewhere when life seemed to feel so much better. It possibly explains why so many people, when faced with an unexpected crisis in their lives, tend to dwell on the past.

Once there is life, there is hope. Without life, there can never be a dream to fulfil, a memory to cherish, a photograph that always makes you smile, or a beautiful scene from nature that takes your breath away as it happens right before your eyes. If you permanently extinguish your life force, you will never bear witness to the future happiness of your children and grandchildren. Life is full of problems; you can sugar-coat them by calling them challenges but at the end of the day they're still problems, though often they can be changed or resolved, managed or overcome, with a little bit of time and insight. When you are suicidal, insight stops working, even though it's pleading with you to just give yourself a chance. Suicide might terminate the invisible pain you have been experiencing relentlessly, but it is also the ultimate form of all endings. It might be impossible to realise the never-ending consequences of your death, but suicide outlives you by clinging forever to the lives of those who loved you, those beautiful lives you left behind. When experiencing suicidal thoughts, it is a good technique to step back from this one-sided pact, and imagine you're watching the two versions of you having this argument as to whether death is worth it, or not. One side of you is determined to end it all; the other side is filled with insight as to why choosing life is the best option.

This simple technique is profoundly life-changing. I have tried it, and I have urged many other people to try it. Once the decision is no longer up to you, because it is being discussed between the 'you' that wants to go, and the 'you' that wants to stay, then your volition or will changes in order to consider other possibilities. When you consider free will, you must take into consideration that your free will is directly linked to the control system in the brain that guides your behaviour. When this control system becomes depressed and anxious, it loses the very control it has been tasked with; it can no longer be relied upon to do its job properly: 'Suicide is the ultimate act of will in a faulty and warped process of self-vindication.'

However, in 2018 I was faced with a totally different dilemma. If I am depressed and, with the professional support that I need to get well and the emotional backing of family and friends, I know I can slowly move my mind and my outlook to a more positive place, then I can eventually learn how to cope with these feelings of despair and hopelessness. But – and this is a big but – if I have been diagnosed with a progressively fatal, incurable illness that is going to leave me physically dependent on someone else for all my daily needs and support, then what's the point of going on? Why would I want to continue to struggle with a life that is slowly breaking down, physically and emotionally – a life that realistically I will have no control over eventually? This is probably the most important question I have raised in my story so far. Its answer has such deep and wide-ranging consequences, not just for me but for the people I love, and rippling out to a much wider circle of people I don't even know who may find themselves in similar circumstances to mine.

In my particular situation though, might dying not seem like a reasonable choice – an escape from an overwhelming and never-ending series of progressively degenerative events? Surely people would understand my choice, given that I was terminally ill and there was no real hope in what lay ahead of me – no contentment, no good health, and no happiness? But that's too much of an assumption. Beyond death there can be no further choices. So I must examine carefully which ones are available to me while I continue to live.

In the weeks after my diagnosis, I realise now as I look back, I was going through a dark night of the soul. The darkness was shocking. I genuinely felt that I was lost forever and would never make it back. I am so relieved I didn't continue to harbour the idea that my life had been left empty of choices and void of joy. It wasn't. Quite the contrary in fact – my life today is wired to resilience and determination. A life-threatening illness still requires a life. The shock of the illness resulted in the death of my ego, not my life that belongs to my beating heart and my conscience. I never had a huge ego; but every life needs a tiny bit of ego to give us confidence in challenging situations. Over time, since my diagnosis and that long dark night of the soul that I believed would never end, I have discovered a new life; you might call it a form of rebirth.

Perhaps there are certain things that do happen for reasons beyond our conscious awareness; perhaps there are forces at work beyond our limited perception that in moments of blinding fear can give us a fleeting glimpse of another option, or make our thought processes less chaotic? For what it's worth, it has always been my belief that it's physically impossible for the human mind to focus on one thought, or to remain in any one state of emotion, for more than a few minutes, maybe even less. Maybe I had just experienced, and not for the first time, the reality of this belief.

The days following my retirement were strange, to put it mildly. As I have mentioned, I had been quite unwell in the preceding months. I knew I couldn't have sustained the workload any longer, so bearing that in mind I suppose my main feeling was one of relief.

Yet in a broader, more profound way, having to say goodbye to my listeners – many of whom had been tuning in to hear me for much of the forty years that I had been a part of their day – was something I found very difficult to deal with. It felt as though I was closing the door on a world that had been 'my place of belonging' for as long as I could remember. There was always something indescribably uplifting about being on radio, playing the music I loved listening to and my listeners loved hearing, while knowing there might be someone out there who'd found strength and hope from something they might have heard during my show on some random afternoon.

I am grateful to have received over the years many emails and handwritten letters from listeners I will never know, telling me that my familiar voice and resilient outlook had made such a difference in their own lives. To those who took the time to write to me – you will never know how much your words meant during difficult times in my life that I couldn't openly talk about while on air.

I must admit there was a novelty about not having to go to work every day. Perhaps this was partly because I worked six days a week for years without taking any substantial breaks during traditional holiday periods, when most people I worked with broke away from their routines and took precious time out. There was a great sense of freedom in not being tied to the same strict routine day in and day out. Life felt looser and I started to feel more relaxed. It also meant I got to spend more time with Paula, without having to rush across Cork city for an early-morning train back to Dublin. It felt as though I was discovering a new healing space that opened up in the middle of a dire crisis.

Chapter 16

MOVING IN TOGETHER

Paula and I had wanted to live together since we first met. Of course it wasn't possible in the early stages. She lived and worked in Cork, and was a busy mother to David and Emma. I lived in Dublin, and the radio station I worked for, Classic Hits, had no permanent facilities in Cork that would enable me to broadcast from there. So, for the first three years, we had no choice but to commit to a long-distance relationship.

Depending on Paula's work schedule, we would alternate our visits to each other at weekends in order to spend as much time as we could together. I would travel to Cork on a Friday evening, returning to Dublin on the Monday morning, and the following weekend Paula would try to organise spending time in Dublin. Of course, as any couple in such a relationship knows, it's never that straightforward – and at times we might go three weeks without seeing each other; on one occasion it was five weeks. Such long periods of time apart can place a huge strain on any relationship but thankfully our marathon phone conversations got us through those days and nights.

Since I was self-employed, there were no allowances for paid holidays or any time off. As a result, the onus was usually on Paula to make the journey to Dublin, which I know can't have been easy – particularly on a Sunday evening, when we would say goodbye to each other and she faced the prospect of the long drive home alone. We both knew that this routine couldn't continue indefinitely.

Within a couple of weeks of my retirement, that sense of isolation set in again. I have always been a private person. I tend to keep to myself. I enjoy my own company, and have no problem whatsoever spending hours alone, maybe reading or writing, or out walking: but this feeling of complete aloneness was like nothing I had ever experienced before. I quickly found myself becoming reclusive. It was as if I was becoming absent from life.

I had a need deep inside me that I felt would never now be fulfilled; perhaps that was because the freedom I always felt was a part of my future was now slowly being taken away from me. I made an appointment with my doctor to chat about it. He explained that there was a strong possibility that I was becoming depressed, which, he reassured me, was not unusual considering the diagnosis I had received. He also reminded me that depression went hand in hand with the slow overall decline that is part of this illness's progression. In addition to all of this was the fact that by this time, severe physical pain was becoming more and more of a permanent fixture in my life. Chronic pain will quickly obscure the mind's ability to think logically. When the pain becomes unbearable, the ability of the mind to remain resilient and defiant collapses. Depending on its severity, pain can make you go mad.

Fortunately, over the weeks that followed, my doctor and my neurologist worked very hard with me to find the right combination of prescription medication that would begin to ease the pain's shocking assault on my body and mind. As the pain became more manageable, thankfully the depression associated with it began to lift.

Almost a month after my retirement, Paula and I decided that the best move for me was to relocate to Cork. She is from Cork, as were many of my ancestors who came mainly from some of the most rural parts that need a good satnav and a savvy local historian to find. Places like Matehy, Dromahane, Nad, and Dripsey; these were the hinterlands of the O'Callaghan clans dating back hundreds of years. Now we were adding another permanent resident to the well-trodden landscape of my forefathers.

We spent two days emptying my small apartment, dumping the hoarded volumes of useless scripts and old newspapers that I had accumulated over the years, careful to keep those that felt like footprints from my radio career, and loading up the car with CDs and as many books as I could take with me. The ones I couldn't find space for went to the local charity shop. I can safely say – hand on heart – I have never thrown out a single book in my life.

Books are like friends, even the ones you've never got around to reading: you respect them and look after them because you never know when you might need to look them up. I'm also acutely aware of the herculean efforts that go into writing a book, especially all those years ago when there were no computers, no 'cut and paste' shortcuts, when books were handwritten, or banged out on an old Olivetti typewriter. As Jane Austen once said, 'The person, be it gentleman or lady, who has not pleasure in a good novel, must be intolerably stupid.' So if the afterlife is where you get to read every book you have ever wanted to read, but never had the time, then I for one will be happy with that.

It felt strange driving away from Dublin that Saturday afternoon: bittersweet memories, away from the city I had been born into and grown up around. I had helped to raise my three young daughters in this town, as I still like to call it. Now they were young adults themselves, finding their own way in life, one of them working in Melbourne at that time, two of them mothers to my beautiful granddaughters. Whenever I think of them, I remember Winnie the Pooh saying that keeping people in your heart means that you're with them forever, even when a time comes that you can't actually be together.

There was a strong hint of 'goodbye, but I'll be back occasionally' in the air that day as we drove south along the M50. Paula and I were finally going to live together, beginning this part of our relationship in the most unanticipated circumstances. I still wonder, three years later, if we would have had this chance in the absence of the diagnosis. If I hadn't become ill, I would no doubt be still working – most likely in Dublin. Would our long-distance relationship have been able to withstand weekend visits for all of that time? I believe it would have survived, considering we've made it this far together despite a very challenging diagnosis.

Instead of the brain-numbing motorways, we decided to take what is affectionately called 'the old road', or the N8, which took us through Durrow, Johnstown and Cashel, and so many small towns and hinterlands that I hadn't travelled through since my days working for RTÉ. We chatted for the entire journey about the future, and what it might or might not throw at us. Of course we were both deeply worried, but we tried to distract ourselves with our Spotify playlists and the conversations that would arise as I passed through many of the towns I hold dear to my heart, thinking back on summer festivals, nightclubs, fundraisers and rugby marquees where I entertained thousands of listeners over the years.

As I watched the miles clock up on the dashboard in front of me, I thought about the years that had passed long before I met Paula, when I was very much single, and how I had come to accept that it was unlikely that I would ever meet someone I would want to spend the rest of my life with. I had imagined that the remaining years would have been spent working and studying. I had even made enquiries about studying law with a view to becoming a barrister. I had contemplated once or twice going back to my therapy practice. But meeting Paula changed all that. Life became filled with a new meaning. Unfortunately life also changed when we found out that I had multiple system atrophy. But we made a promise to each other a few months after the shock of the diagnosis had passed, that we would never allow this illness to come between us.

Our three-hour trek south that afternoon was filled with music and chat, but never far from moments of poignant reminiscing and the anticipation of all that lay ahead. That day, when I left my native city behind to be with the woman I had fallen in love with barely three years before, neither of us had any idea what our future held.

Chapter 17

THE HEALING GRIEF

Grief can often be the most challenging aspect of living with a chronic illness. It's like having no choice but to follow a path you never knew existed, through a strange and harsh landscape, rocky and uncharted, that takes you away from the everyday life that was once familiar to you. This landscape allows you rare glimpses of how life used to be. Others will reassure you that they are travelling the new road with you, but in reality they can't, because they are still grounded in what was once your own familiar world. When you have a chronic, incurable illness, there's a need to grieve the past; in the same way that losing a loved one creates a yearning to relive the past when life was spent together. I could never have known it three years ago, but grief turns to growth; but it can be a painful growth that so often feels almost impossible to stay the distance with.

I felt this stifling grief long after I had left the Mater. It's as though time gives you a chance to adjust in some psychological way to life after hospital, after hearing your diagnosis, before it pours this intense sorrow on you, like getting caught in a torrential downpour. It just hits you so hard. I remember the day it first hit me.

I was on air one Sunday morning, almost a month after I had come home from hospital. I played a song by the band Alphaville, called 'Forever Young', a favourite of mine for over thirty years. Its lyrics and the power of the accompaniment hit me unexpectedly hard that morning, as I listened to Marian Gold's soaring voice, even though I had played it thousands of times. It was as though I was hearing it for the very first time. That line about hoping for the best but expecting the worst reminded me of what my neurologist had said to me the week before I was admitted for the final tests. It was a moment I will never forget. I couldn't move as a result of this feeling of deep and poignant distress. This song was linking me to a life that existed somewhere in the 'before' years.

'Forever Young' took me in an instant to a time in my life that was filled with people I hadn't thought of in years. As the chorus soars in Gold's voice, I can see myself waving to my family from the railings of the car ferry as I leave Ireland to begin a life in England in the mid-1980s, as a young DJ hungry to advance my career and be the best I could be. As I listened to it I also became a young father again for the briefest of moments, telling my daughters – as we made banana sandwiches on a Saturday night to eat while watching An American Tale – that this was a song all about being young and having your whole life to look forward to.

That Sunday morning the song's lyrics suddenly tasted of bittersweet regret, a longing in my heart to turn back the years and find the moment when this illness planted its very first seeds in me. My grief didn't need a starting point, because it had visited me before, wearing many faces. I turned the speakers in the studio to their highest volume and listened. The song is about living life to its fullest and seizing the chances we are given to be our very best at whatever we do, and to make the most of every moment we have, because it can all be taken away without warning. It's a song I still go back to late some nights, when I want to be reminded of what it felt like – as every one of us has at some point in our lives – to be forever young.

Grief is a lonely business. We're encouraged to talk about our grief; but that grief is the type we feel following the death of a friend or a loved one. Who can you turn to when the grief you are experiencing is for yourself, nursing the pain of those personal losses that no one else can see? You're grieving your own death, even though you're not yet dead. It's difficult to explain this frame of mind to someone who has not experienced chronic illness. Grieving is very different from wallowing in self-pity. Trust me, if you have a chronic, incurable illness you are perfectly entitled to feel sorry for yourself. Immerse yourself in the distress you feel, face it in the mirror. It's perfectly fine to feel angry and bitter. This heavy heart, this melancholia, is your grief, so claim it. If you feel like having the occasional morning to 'self-wallow', then make it worth your while: get out into nature, sit among trees, take some time to listen to water flowing, knowing that a flowing river never stops, just like a beating heart enduring its own secret grief. You are entitled to it; don't ever let anyone try to change it from what it is.

To those who might say to you, 'Stop using your illness as an excuse,' whatever that illness might be, you might consider replying with, 'Why don't you stop using my illness as your excuse?' But then you realise they are trying to spare themselves from the grief that still calls out to them even though they are trying their hardest to keep it at a distance. It's their grief that is resonating with yours. If they truly love you and want to care about you, then they'll be comfortable expressing this grief they feel for you. Or maybe they won't want to tell you. They might even build an invisible wall to protect themselves from feeling the pain they know is inside them, afraid to let it out because they don't know what to say to you. But you can't wait for them to come around to that realisation. You must move on through your grief, often alone.

Elisabeth Kübler-Ross, a Swiss-American psychiatrist, wrote a book in 1969 called *On Death and Dying*, which became one of the biggest sellers of its time. How can a book that talks about grief become so popular? It's because grief is so personal, it's almost impossible to have a conversation about it. Grief is a difficult bridge to cross. Not everyone makes it to the far side. Her book discussed the path that the five stages of grief follow: disbelief, anger, bargaining, depression and, finally, acceptance.

Since my diagnosis, I have come to identify with all of these stages. However, grief does not align itself into such clearly defined phases. They don't all queue up in an orderly line. They become absorbed into your mind and body, and you feel like you are going mad. You don't have to be mourning death (in the literal sense) to experience these profoundly confusing and unsettling states of being. Grief is messy and rotten. It feels like having the flu but not having a bed to lie on. You can be mourning the death of your own self-intimacy that no longer gives you the warmth and inner sense of belonging that brought you comfortably home to yourself in private moments of ease and contentment. All of that is gone. You are in a mess. It's very hard to see how the last phase, acceptance, can ever find its way into the melting pot.

I don't subscribe to the 'five stages of grief' plan. Grief is like landing in a different country and realising you don't speak the language. You move around, you spend some time here and there, and then you find yourself washed up on some beach somewhere and you don't know how you got there.

But where – if ever – does the journey end?

The order of grieving, when you see it described in such rational terms, is regarded as the traditional path that one takes through grief of any kind. However, it's both clichéd and unhelpful to assume there is anything prescribed about grief. It comes in its own time, not necessarily when you expect it or want it to come, and it stays within you, accompanied by waves of beautiful memories, and a hunger for the past to return so that everything can be exactly as it was during those happier times. Grief can be a calm moment of realisation, or it can be so emotionally destructive that you feel as though you are helpless in the face of loss and might not survive the journey. Grief must become a part of you so that you can navigate this bleak landscape and find some sort of way – any way – to move forward, while still allowing the loss you are feeling to pass right through you. This allows you to live with grief, rather than constantly trying to run away from it.

The journey each of us takes once we find out we have a chronic illness must not be allowed to become simply a journey of grief. That only serves to invite more pain and isolation and helplessness. Since my diagnosis, I've learned that this new journey must have a purpose.

The 'Forever Young' song taught me that there is a place inside me where I can be whatever I want to be and no one has to give me approval. If I find inner strength by believing that I can be forever young, then my heart and mind will thank me for it.

Grieving can be one of the most painful journeys we ever have to take, but it can also be one of the most enriching times of our lives. I can honestly say that I have learned more about who I really am in the last three years than I have in three decades. I think that's because a health scare, with all the uncertainty that it brings, tends to cut through the chaff and garbage that weighs you down in normal times. Grief makes you painfully honest. My tolerance levels dropped; my boredom threshold went through the floor. I have become choosy about my time, and how and with whom I want to spend it.

I wasn't turning my back on the world as I emerged from this period of grief; I still very much wanted to be a part of it, but on my terms. You can still be generous with your time, and reach out to those who need and love you, but you also need to reach inwards to yourself. Sometimes it's good to warm your own heart by doing something that makes you happy. I found I needed to be kinder to myself. I needed to listen to that soft voice that wants to talk to me regularly, the voice of my heart. It's only there in the silence, so I have to put aside time so that I can engage it. It doesn't speak to me in words, but I know when I need to listen to its sentiments.

Another thing I've learned through this grieving stage is the healing power of spending time in nature. I've started to love myself more, but only because I feel at home with myself when I am close to tall old trees that have lived this journey longer than I have, and take forest walks, and stroll by the sea, when I can feel the power of the waves on a windswept day as they pound down onto the sand with the incoming tide. These are the beauties of life that I have taken for granted for years, but now form a central part of who I am becoming.

Why do we spend so much of our lives beating ourselves up, carrying this weight of unworthiness around inside us? I can only speak for myself when I say I did it all my life. I'm still working hard on changing how I feel about myself. I remind myself to be more gentle, more in tune with the inner world rather than a world that continues whether we want to be part of it or not. It's a work in progress, but I'm not in any rush.

I know there are many types of grief, and I'm not

for a minute saying that any type of bereavement grieving is enriching, but the power of grief cannot be separated from the power of life; it is not a standalone emotion. It needs its own human emotions to feed into. It colours everything it feeds into, every feeling and every experience. Grief is about coming to terms with living in a world that has changed for me without my permission; it's a juggling act that balances precariously between finding a way to live with myself in this new harsh environment of emotional disorientation, while trying to continue to be the same person I once was for those who love me and want me to be fine. But I can see now that grief has become more about learning to cope with life, than dealing with loss. By spending too much time dealing with loss, we lose sight of the importance of finding a new purpose. The old purposes belong to the old world we are leaving behind us. They quickly lose their value, washed away by the grief that accompanies serious illness. A new purpose gives us the resilience to find a new direction going forward. Only then will the journey restore hope to our lives.

Chapter 18

ANGER AND THE
QUEST FOR PURPOSE

One of the most difficult aspects of living with illness is finding meaning in your life, a purpose that is relevant in terms of where you find yourself now, while also facing up to the ongoing changes within you that you have little if any control over.

Serious illness often requires us to adopt a twin-track existence, almost like leading a double life. One of those lives is the sick one, where you're trying to cope with the pain, fear and uncertainty you feel every day, attending appointments, learning to cope, and praying to get well again; the other life is the one that people who know you well want to share with you. They don't want you to change, despite your illness. They urge you on, encouraging you to stay strong. They want you to be normal, to be as well as you can be. It's not their intention to try to reduce the severity of your condition, or to mollify you in any way. They still want to meet you, to have conversations with you, to catch up on life, to hear your voice and your laughter, to know that you're doing your best to beat the odds. They know the importance of routine, and so they encourage you to keep going. It's as important for you as it is for them, even though there are times when you can barely cope with your own company.

Clothes need to be washed and dried. Once the diagnosis honeymoon has come to an end, it's more or less back to business as usual. Other people's lives will continue as they always have, and many of those diagnosed with chronic illness have to walk that thin line between 'I have no energy to work' and 'I have no choice but to work'. But eventually you reach the point where you are physically unable to work.

For months after my diagnosis, I experienced some really bad days, emotionally and physically. In the immediate aftermath of learning about my illness, my life felt as though it was falling apart. Each new day would present something that I hadn't expected, whether that was anger, or sadness, or nausea caused by the medication. I was on so much medication that I would sometimes accidentally take an extra pill, forgetting that I had already taken one an hour before. Depending on what the tablets were for, my body would react in different ways, but mostly with chronic nausea, and having to go back to bed for the rest of the day. Sadness was something I dragged around quite a lot. I could mostly handle that, but the one emotion that took me by surprise and frightened me more than any other was anger.

I will never forget the afternoon Paula and I left my neurologist's office, having been told that I would be admitted to hospital the following Tuesday for a fortnight of tests. Towards the end of our appointment, the neurologist explained that he had eliminated almost all of the other illnesses that I was being checked out for; that left only one. It was the illness Paula and I had prayed we would never have to face up to, but here it was being laid out in front of us. Paula would tell me later what his exact words were because all I heard was the sound of an ambulance's siren getting nearer and then passing by the window outside. 'We're looking at the possibility of multiple system atrophy.' He didn't take his eyes off his notes.

I squeezed Paula's hand. She began to cry. I was sitting beside her in a t-shirt and a pair of briefs, nothing else, following a long litany of clinical tests that he wanted to carry out again just to be certain that he had covered all possibilities. I could feel my cheeks turn roaring red. My ears felt as though they were on fire. My hands and legs started to tremble. I couldn't breathe. I tried to catch my breath but couldn't.

The neurologist stood up and walked around the desk. He placed his hand on my shoulder. 'I'll give you a few moments,' he said, then left the room.

I wasn't sure if that was to allow me get dressed,

or to give me time to cry. I didn't cry as I pulled on my jeans and trainers. I was more concerned about Paula. Tears streamed down her cheeks and she couldn't catch her breath. I didn't bother with my socks, shoving my shoelaces into each shoe because I couldn't remember how to tie them. My name is Gareth, I said to myself. I couldn't breathe. I needed the air outside. The room was beginning to get smaller and my head felt light. 'Let's get out of here,' I said to Paula. It was the first moment I felt the anger rising up inside me.

We pulled the building's huge Georgian door closed behind us and stood on the top step, holding hands. I could feel the heat of the sun against my forehead, yet my body was freezing. Was I in shock? I pulled my jacket close around me. People across the street were wearing light summer clothes, showing off their white shoulders to the hot sun; sunglasses were everywhere. One man was eating an ice cream as he held his young son's hand. People seemed to be happy. Why were they happy? Their happiness just seemed all so wrong. 'Fuck happiness. Stop being happy,' I wanted to scream at the top of my voice.

'Where will we go?' Paula asked me, not letting go of my hand.

I nodded to the main entrance of the Mater Private Hospital across the street. 'Let's go over there. We'll get a coffee.' But I didn't want a coffee. I didn't want anything. I wanted to run away from this strange street, full of private consultancy clinics for sick people. I wanted to be told there'd been a mistake. I wanted to hear that I didn't have MSA. A taxi driver beeped his horn at us as we crossed the busy street. He shouted something at me through the open window. I told him to fuck off. Anger, so much anger in me, and there was even more as we walked towards the hospital entrance. I pounded my feet on the pavement. I wanted to kick the rubbish bin beside the bus stop. People seemed to be staring at us. Why? Could they tell I was ranting? What was I saying? I could hear my voice but it didn't sound like I was saying anything. A patient sat on the hospital windowsill in the sunshine in her dressing gown, smoking a cigarette, inhaling deeply and coughing profusely as she exhaled the smoke into *my* space, obviously a lifelong smoker with her facial wrinkling and bad complexion. I was so angry. I felt like screaming at her, 'What are you doing? You're an inpatient in a private fucking hospital. You probably have some serious illness and here you are ... out here on the street smoking?' We walked into the hospital foyer. I was out of breath, hyperventilating, looking for a hand sanitiser. I spotted one but there was a man standing in front of it on his phone. I stared at him until he moved. The machine was empty. I wanted to rip the useless bottle off its wall attachment. So much anger, heart pounding, eyes watering up, too many people crowding my space, and I felt as though I was about to explode. We walked outside again into the sunshine.

Paula called my boss and explained that I wouldn't be coming into work that day. I could hear him telling her that I was due on air in less than two hours. Then I could hear the anger in her voice, not unlike mine, 'He won't be in. He's just been diagnosed with a terminal illness, for God's sake!'

The only way to get rid of the anger you're feeling because you've just found out that there's a strong likelihood that you're terminally ill is to drink alcohol, which we did for the remainder of the day.

As we sat in a Wetherspoon's in Blanchardstown, it dawned on me that everything had changed, in the space of a few moments earlier that afternoon, when I was told my life was going to be altered forever by a horrible, incurable illness. How can anyone be the same after being told this? How dare the world go on as if nothing has happened. A bunch of middle-aged men with beer bellies sat around a table next to us, engrossed in a football match on a big screen in the corner of the pub, as though their lives depended on the outcome. I wanted to scream at them, tell them to get up off their lazy arses and do something worthwhile with their lives. So much anger built up inside, and nothing to take it away.

For weeks following that day, I couldn't listen to the radio. I couldn't allow myself to play my favourite songs. No music, no familiar voices, nothing in the car, or in the apartment at home, but silence. I needed perfect silence. It was the only place where the anger couldn't find me.

My old life no longer interested me. It was dead.

I took days off work; then the days would turn into a full week. I didn't feel well. It probably wasn't the illness much of the time; I was just sick of life. My life was sick and I was sick of life. My boss told me one day, 'You should be working; you really need to be here at work, instead of being on your own. It's not good for your health.'

The anger would rise up inside as I listened to his words. 'How dare you suggest your advice over what I want for me,' I could hear myself shouting at him in my head, as I listened to him trying to reason with me. 'Why should I go back to work to suit you and not what I want for myself?' I could hear that inner voice shouting, drowning out his words. 'What do you care about my health for? You just want me back because you're afraid your business will lose money if I'm not working!'

People were telling me to stay active. Why? They had no idea what sort of pain I was in, or how depleted my energy was, or how pissed off and fed up with life I felt. I hated hearing those words. Bloody moral high ground windbags with their clichéd advice, even though most of them didn't really give a shit about me; all those people who barely knew me telling me to *stay active*. Why should I stay active? What good was that going to do me? Staying active wasn't going to cure me. I would have preferred them to say, 'Now the best thing you could do is go to the pub and get drunk.' It was all anger inside me that wanted to explode, but I daren't let it show because it terrified me, I realise now; such a stifling angry reaction to an illness I didn't deserve.

In the last few weeks of my radio career, the shows felt flat in my ears. I struggled so hard to sound upbeat and positive. I wanted to be able to believe that I could still do this because it brought happiness to others; but the happiness it had brought me for years was gone. It had packed up and left and I knew for certain it wasn't coming back. I was witnessing a rare occurrence: I had outlived my purpose. I would have these recurring dreams where I was sitting in the studio but the room and the equipment had shrunk, and my fingers were too big and clumsy to work the tiny buttons and knobs; and the studio chair was too small to sit on. It was the unconscious mind's way of telling me I'd outgrown my purpose; time to go now.

Surely there can't be only one purpose in life, I asked myself on the rare days I would walk along the bank of the Royal Canal towards the city, just to get out of my small apartment and remind myself that the world was getting on without me. You've stepped off, pal. The rest of them have moved on. Was radio really the *only* purpose in my life? I started to think that it was. My three daughters were adults now, two of them busy mammies, and my third girl was half a world away in Australia. I had outgrown the hands-on responsibilities and commitments of being a father. I was now on the second tier of parenthood, in a kind of secondary role, looking in at these busy young women getting on with their lives, as I'm sure my own parents did when I was a young father with small children.

So what then was my purpose going to be from now on? I needed a purpose, a reason to get out of bed in the mornings. My radio days were over. Even if I hadn't been struck down by this progressive illness, I was definitely into the final stages of a career that doesn't have many openings for a bloke who's almost sixty. Radio had become a very different vehicle to the one I had hopped a ride on forty years before.

Viktor Frankl, in his ground-breaking book *Man's*

Search for Meaning, says, 'When we are no longer able to change a situation – just think of an incurable disease such as inoperable cancer – we are challenged to change ourselves.' Frankl was imprisoned in Auschwitz as a young man, where he dug and laid rail tracks that carried thousands of Jews to the gas chambers. Over the course of three years, Frankl was moved between four concentration camps. His brother and mother died at Auschwitz; his wife died at Bergen-Belsen. As a long-time prisoner, Frankl found himself stripped to naked existence. His father also died in one of the camps. Except for his sister, his entire family perished. He always stressed that the true meaning of life is to be discovered in the world rather than within ourselves. He calls this characteristic 'the self-transcendence of human existence'.

I had bought his book many years ago while studying psychotherapy, but – as is so often the case – I really only began to make sense of his theories shortly after my own diagnosis. How many of us can honestly imagine what life in the concentration camps must have been like, and the constant fear that you could die at any moment. But Frankl believed that life still had a meaning and that suffering had a purpose, despite the savagery of the prisoners' conditions. While it was virtually impossible to escape physically, he believed that each of us could escape even the most unbearable conditions through our spiritual selves. Frankl believed that the spiritual self could not be affected by external forces.

So much of what Frankl preached in the decades after his release made perfect sense to me during my coming to terms with my illness, but also in the last year as we have adjusted to living with COVID-19. Frankl believed that real purpose – which makes life worth living – can only be found through creativity, interacting with other like-minded individuals instead of isolating ourselves, and, most importantly, in the way in which we respond to inevitable suffering.

I have discovered over the last three years that suffering does not signal an end to life; if anything it creates a greater urgency to live what's left of that life to its fullest. Without suffering, life can become complacent, even dull and boring. I'm not suggesting that each of us needs to physically suffer in order to realise the true meaning of life, but suffering does quickly strip away the ego that prevents us from discovering our true purpose. Physical and emotional suffering is an enormous challenge. It tests us to the very core. It quickly locates our true worth. Such a challenge, while not remotely pleasant, can cause a transformation we never thought possible. It has certainly taught me about who I really am, and, more importantly, all the things I'm not.

Brian Keenan, the Belfast-born teacher and writer of *An Evil Cradling*, said in an interview with the London *Independent* in 2004, 'If courage is about anything, it is about knowing that everything is within yourself.' Brian was kidnapped in Beirut in 1986 and held captive in a prison cell by Islamic Jihad for four and a half years. I have always hugely admired him, and since my diagnosis, Keenan's experiences at the hands of his kidnappers have taught me a valuable lesson. Although serious illness might take away my freedom at some point in its relentless progression, it might lock up and distort my physical body and disable its natural ability to express itself as it has done all its life, it can never take away my liberty. My liberty is the untouchable energy that exists within me, the spirit that can never be silenced, that breathes life into my self-understanding. It might rob my voice and my physical exterior that people recognise, but it can never rob my spirit. Could this be my new purpose in life? Perhaps it is.

Phil first came to see me when I was working as a therapist. He was fifty-two. He suffered from chronic anxiety and periods of depression which he assumed were symptoms of his unhappy marriage. Less than a month after his divorce, Phil got some very bad news. He was diagnosed with an extremely rare form of cancer, called mesothelioma: a highly aggressive form of the disease that affects the linings of the lungs and chest wall. As cancers go, it doesn't get much worse. Such a diagnosis is one of those 'get your affairs in order' moments.

Phil's divorce had dragged on for years, during which time he lost every cent of savings he had worked hard for all his life. Two of his four children, who were all grown adults by then, didn't talk to him, even though he had been a loving and providing father all his life.

He called and gave me the news: 'I'm dying. There's nothing they can do for me.'

We met later that evening, and I explained to him that while, yes, there was little his oncologist could do for him, there was lots he could do for himself. Phil's greatest fear was that he wouldn't get to see his three grandchildren before he died. The refusal of two of his children to talk to him meant he hadn't seen his grandsons in four years.

'How long have they given you?' I asked him.

'The consultant told me I probably have six months.'

'But that's all based on pathological evidence and prognostic statistics,' I explained to him. It was time to get rid of the old homeostasis and build a new one. Homeostasis, as I mentioned earlier, is a biological force that acts to keep things in balance, and restore them when they have been upset.

Over the following days, we discussed various options, and the importance of finding a new purpose that would remove him from the paralysing fear of this illness. One of those was the health benefits of getting a dog. Of course, Phil accepted that he was too far advanced in his illness to bring home a small puppy and train him and rear him into adulthood and beyond. So he decided to apply to become a volunteer puppy raiser, for the Irish Guide Dogs association.

Phil's role would involve house-training, grooming, and basic obedience exercises, and all going well, Phil's puppy would then advance to more complex training and eventually pass all the tests to become a guide dog. Having been matched with Phil, Ben the Labrador, who had just turned three, settled into his new home.

Phil and Ben got on famously. One was never seen without the other. Phil outlived the six-month prognosis and, despite the occasional tough days involving treatment, I began to see a youthfulness develop in him that I had never witnessed before. He called me one evening to tell me proudly that his daughters had arrived for dinner with his grandsons. I had never heard him so happy. His grandsons fell in love with Ben; so much so, that they spent most weekends staying with their grandad and his super dog.

After twenty-two months, Ben was ready to graduate as a fully trained assistance dog, and was matched with his new owner, Aaron, an eleven-year-old boy with autism. Naturally Phil found it very difficult saying goodbye to Ben, but there was contentment and a sense of achievement about him that I will never forget. His time spent with Ben had become his new homeostasis. He told me that it had been one of his greatest purposes in life.

Almost eight weeks later, one of Phil's daughters phoned me to say that her dad had passed away peacefully that morning, surrounded by his children and their partners. They played his favourite song, 'He Ain't Heavy, He's My Brother,' to him during his final moments.

On the morning of his funeral, the sun shone brightly as Phil's family and his many friends turned out to pay their own personal tributes to a wonderful, much-loved man. His daughters had asked that Ben the Labrador be allowed to attend. It was a poignant scene to watch Ben, and his owner Aaron, proudly leading the way ahead of Phil's coffin to his final resting place in the local cemetery, overlooking the sea that he had loved so much all his life.

One of his daughters shook my hand and gave me an envelope as everyone was leaving the church. 'Dad asked me to give you this.' It read:

Dear Gareth,

Sometimes it takes bad news to make you realise just how special life can be. When I was told I was dying, my life fell apart. But if my life hadn't fallen apart, I would never have been given the chance to fulfil the dream of a lifetime, namely to help someone like Aaron, and to reconcile with my children. Thanks to Ben, I got to achieve my dream, and now Ben is helping Aaron to achieve all of his dreams.

Bad news, I've learned, can lead to good news. Sometimes when we face into our toughest challenge, we are also setting out on a path that gives us hope, despite the bad news. It took Ben to teach me there is hope in the unknown. Never give up. If I had given up, who knows what might never have happened.

Thank you.

See you down the road.

Your friend, Phil

Having a purpose is so important because it gives you an identity that is unique to you. Right now one of my most important purposes in life is to complete this book. It has been my focus for almost two years. It had been floating around inside my mind, taking shape in dozens of notebooks, for years before that. It was only when I received my diagnosis that I felt I needed more than ever to write it. At the start, my reason for writing it was because I wanted to be remembered after I died. Being told you have an incurable illness that will progress until it kills you creates an urgency to do things that will preserve your legacy, and help those who love you to remember you – your writings, your voice, your laughter, your pictures, your music. As time goes on, and you realise that you're still very much alive, you tend to back down from the 'I'm possibly going to die soon' frame of mind.

Once this book is published, I intend to start work on another. My editor expects that I won't be happy with just two books, so she's already cleared a small shelf in her office. Ah … so there's my purpose; well, one of them. My central purpose gives a full and spiritual value to my life, whatever that might be. Could it be my writing? I love words, and how they resonate with my readers. It's easy to talk; it's not so easy to write it down and make it public. My mother loves her gardening and does it every opportunity she gets. It's both spiritual and fulfilling and gives a special purpose to her day. Another purpose she finds so important to her life is her strong faith. She feels her day is not complete without a visit to her local church, where she lights candles for all of us and prays for our many intentions. Her faith fills her life with meaning and purpose.

I love the prospect of driving to the coast. I relish the thought of walking the beach at Garretstown, or nearby Coolmaine, for miles, no matter what the weather holds; I find an ancient graveyard, or I stand at the edge of a cliff and stare out at the sea as it stretches for miles to where it meets the skyline. These meanderings remind me that my purpose is to be here, to be present, and to make myself a full and active part of this life. I wrote earlier about grief, the type of grief that can flatten us when we find out we have a serious illness. The longer we grieve, the more we become trapped within ourselves, trapped without ever hoping to find a purpose.

Whenever I stand on the beach these days, I take plenty of time to stare out at the horizon. I realise now that in order to find a new purpose in life, it's so important for each of us to look beyond our old defunct horizon. I ask myself the question, 'What lies beyond it?' To see beyond the old horizon is to spiritually commit to a new purpose in life, whatever that might be. We can never close our eyes to new horizons.

Anyone who has Parkinson's disease will tell you that the part of the brain that is responsible for the production of dopamine becomes impaired as a result, and this causes major problems with mobility, along with a long list of other internal symptoms that become more difficult to manage as the disease progresses. Most Parkinson's patients take a medication called levodopa, which is converted to dopamine once it crosses the blood-brain barrier. This generic form of dopamine continues to support the body's need for this neurotransmitter so that the nastier symptoms involving impaired movement and co-ordination can be kept at bay for as long as possible.

This is where it becomes interesting for those of us who have multiple system atrophy. I have a Parkinson's form of MSA, known as MSA-P. This means that while the illness continues along its own strange and unpredictable trajectory, I share most symptoms that someone with Parkinson's disease will experience. Therefore I also take levodopa, which is being converted into dopamine in my brain and benefiting my movement and my balance, like it does for most Parkinson's patients. Unfortunately, many sufferers of MSA do not react favourably – in many cases there is no reaction at all – to levodopa.

One of the main neurological tests for multiple system atrophy involves giving the patient very high dosages of levodopa. If the levodopa shows no beneficial results in easing the physical symptoms of the disease, then a diagnosis of MSA is mostly favoured. It's well-known that many neurologists adopt a 'wait and see' approach to deciding on a specific diagnosis. This is because so many of the Parkinson-ism illnesses are almost identical to Parkinson's disease in their early developmental stages. Parkinson's mostly reacts positively to levodopa, whereas multiple system atrophy does not in most cases.

However – and herein is the great inconsistency

in deciding whether it's Parkinson's or MSA – some patients with MSA *do* react favourably to levodopa. Could I be one of those patients? Does this mean, because levodopa is converted to dopamine in my brain even though my diagnosis is not Parkinson's, that my deterioration is slower and my decline in health is more gradual than for those MSA patients who cannot take levodopa, for whatever reason?

You cannot allow yourself to become a prisoner of an illness, no matter what that illness is called. It's just a name that differentiates it from other illnesses, no matter how serious and life-threatening it may seem to be. You can give up, or you can fight on; that is the choice each of us faces. Excuses to give up are more persuasive when your brain has formed a habit of thinking negatively.

As I continue to remind myself and those few who listen to me, there is always hope in the unknown. However, in order to truly believe this, and live that belief every day, you have to choose freedom over conformity. To conform is to adapt to being told by someone else what you should do, instead of listening to that inner voice that reminds you that if you can't find any hope in the familiar and the acceptable, then look for hope in the unknown. If the conventional route isn't working, look for those who have found healing by choosing a path that's different.

A man is walking home one night when he sees his neighbour crawling around on his hands and knees searching frantically under a street lamp for something on the ground.

'What have you lost?' the man asks.

'I'm looking for my keys,' the neighbour replies anxiously.

'Here, let me help you,' the man says. Soon both men are on their knees under the streetlight, looking for the keys. After an hour the man asks his neighbour, 'Where exactly did you lose the keys?'

The neighbour waves his hand back towards the darkness. 'Over there inside my house,' he replies.

The man jumps up and scratches his head in frustration. 'Then why are you searching for your keys here, if you lost them inside your house?'

'Because there is more light here than inside my house,' the neighbour replies casually.

This story is almost one thousand years old. It's

what's known as a metaphor. The keys, or answers, are to be found in our house, or within ourselves – a dark and confusing place to find answers, but we need to keep searching. It's so much easier to look outside ourselves in the light where we'll see all the things that look like the solution we're searching for, such as false hope, insincerity, material things, and other people's beliefs and opinions.

In this chapter I have explored the life-saving importance of finding a central purpose in life. We can have many purposes, but unless there is one in particular that we feel naturally endeared to, one that gives our life a real sense of calling, or mission, then our internal environment – namely our health – will not be in sync with our external environment, and we will become unwell. It's only a matter of time. So it's important that we challenge ourselves to find our purpose sooner rather than putting it on the long finger. Call it a mission statement. It could be learning web design, discovering how to paint with oils on canvas, or even studying the enriching lives of trees. These are just three I mention here because I have added them to my own bucket list of mission statements. The options are endless. Make your own list. Don't be afraid to challenge yourself. The main thing to remember is that purpose and homeostasis are directly linked. If your mission statement takes you to a state where you are so completely absorbed by what you are doing that you don't notice time slipping by, then your body and mind will reward you richly with homeostasis.

Chapter 19

GIVE-UP-ITIS AND
THE JOY OF SINGING

A recent survey of a thousand people found that more than ninety percent ranked doctors as the most trusted professionals. I wouldn't expect it to be any other way. However, another study showed that many people hesitate to ask questions of their doctor for fear of being labelled difficult. Even though many patients – if not most – want to share in the decision-making process, they do not always speak up.

When it comes to illness, we rely heavily on what doctors tell us. We rarely question their opinion, and nearly always accept their decisions and directions. If we feel unwell, we make an appointment to see our doctor. I get to sit in front of my doctor for twenty minutes, during which time I expect him to examine me, reach a conclusion on why I am feeling unwell, and then medicate, by way of a prescription for my local chemist.

Many people prefer to leave all the difficult decisions about their medical care in the hands of their doctor, while some even prefer not to be told any specific details about what lies ahead, and only to be given information on a need-to-know basis. I know of one man who received a very difficult diagnosis, and would only deal with his doctor through his wife. The results of any tests he needed to undergo would be sent to her; he didn't want to know what the results were unless they brought good news. He died soon after his diagnosis.

Retired American surgeon Bernie Siegel has written many books on the relationship between the patient and the healing process. When discussing why some patients were determined to fight their illness, while others just turned towards the wall and died, he said in his book *Love, Medicine and Miracles*, 'Long-term survivors had poor relationships with their physicians – as judged by the physicians. They asked a lot of questions and expressed their emotions freely.'

I ask my doctor a *lot* of questions whenever I feel the need to pay him a visit. I have known Michael for most of my adult life. While I trust his judgement, I'm not reluctant to ask the difficult questions. Doctors *don't* get embarrassed. Most doctors expect you to ask questions. They're trained to understand how and why embarrassing things happen to our bodies, so if I don't ask the question, how can I expect to get the answer I need?

While on the subject, something else I cannot emphasise enough is the importance of doing your own research before you visit your doctor. I hear so many professionals saying, 'Don't google!' I disagree. What I don't agree with is self-diagnosing. That's just gambling with your health. The internet is filled with insightful, clinical knowledge from highly reputable and respectable sources. These sources are easy to find if you spend a little time searching carefully.

I have learned so much from people I have met over the years – people who have overcome the most challenging situations I can think of. One man I know who was diagnosed with inoperable cancer and told he had less than a year to live decided, against the advice of his family, to join the local choir. He is still singing two years later and only last night called me to see if I had finished writing this book. He asked me if, once I had finished, I would like to join his choir. Could this be another purpose to enrich the quality and value of my life? I would think so. I told him I would have to see if I had the time. I've never been as busy as I am right now and I wouldn't want to commit myself if it meant letting these singers down. What a wonderful complaint to have, I thought; I'm too busy doing things that I love. I have purpose in my life. I asked him about his cancer. 'The specialist doesn't want to see me until next March,' he replied.

A purpose that resonates at the deepest level of our being brings us right back to something I mentioned earlier – the state of homeostasis, where the body and mind are balanced and in harmony.

Music has a direct connection to homeostasis. There have been thousands of books written about the power of music and its ability to heal and to create shifts within the brain that conventional medication can't do. It is now known that different types of music can cause positive healing reactions within regions of the brain that years ago we would never have imagined was possible.

One of the best examples of this is the video posted by a Spanish charity, Asociacion Musica para Despertar (Music Association for Awakening), which uses music to improve the lives of dementia patients. The video went viral within hours of being posted online. It shows Alzheimer's patient Martina Gonzalez, a former ballerina, who is completely transformed, and starts to recall and then mimic some of her old choreography moves as she listens to a recording of Tchaikovsky's *Swan Lake*. The former lead dancer sprang into action, immediately remembering the routine she performed over fifty years ago as she listened to the evocative piece. She spent her final days in a care home in Valencia and passed away in 2019 shortly after the video was recorded.

You will know by now that I have loved music for as long as I can remember, but I also love to sing. I am that motorist you notice in the car beside you, while you're waiting for the traffic lights to turn green, who sits behind the wheel oblivious to everything but the music, with the stereo volume turned up. Singing out loud and driving on an empty open road is pure therapy and escapism. It's one of life's guilty pleasures.

It's not something I do often when I'm out in public, say while sitting on a bus, or wandering around the supermarket. However, if you call to our front door most evenings, the likelihood is you will find me sitting at our kitchen table holding a microphone and singing at the top of my voice to backing tracks of my favourite songs.

I'm often reminded that I'm not the only singer in our house. It's usually at that point that Paula takes the microphone from me and quickly outshines my efforts with her pitch-perfect voice. Occasionally we sing duets; trying to harmonise on some of our songs.

Sometimes it works. Of course, a couple of drinks always help to loosen the vocal chords.

For me, singing is the best form of speech and language therapy I can think of. Speech therapists have long waiting lists, and time is not a friend of my disabling illness. One of the tragic symptoms of multiple system atrophy is losing your voice. I try every day to keep my voice strong and consistent. It has been my livelihood for forty years. I can never imagine not being able to speak and sing. It's just too shocking to even think about it. My medical team are quite surprised that my voice remains so strong this long after my diagnosis. Perhaps it's because I have used it so consistently for so long throughout my career on the radio. Who knows how long I will get to keep it. I can only hope it's for a long time to come. And so I sing at every opportunity I get. I decided I had to do it the only way I knew best. It's how we spend our evenings – singing; in the same way that others watch television, play cards, go to the movies, or go for a run. Some people invest in a treadmill. We went out and bought ourselves a karaoke machine.

Whenever I hear someone say they don't have a favourite song, or they 'don't have time' to listen to music, I always feel like telling them that music is one of life's greatest gifts. Friedrich Nietzsche explained it perfectly: 'Without music, life would be a mistake.' I have always believed that the key to a woman's heart is hidden in her playlist; Paula and I have compiled many such playlists together. If I am going to lose my voice to this illness, then it's going to have to put up one hell of a fight to take it from me.

According to a recent study, music performance by professional musicians enhanced the activity of genes involved in dopaminergic neurotransmission, motor behaviour, memory, and learning. Basically by singing regularly we function more efficiently. I can vouch for that. After spending an hour singing some of my favourite songs, I feel energised and elated. Music performance is known to cause structural and functional changes to the human brain, while also enhancing cognition. So why aren't we all singing more often?

Some years back, I was invited to give a talk to a large group of people on depression, and how they needed to find ways to overcome it. I was introduced by my host and took my place on the stage. I looked around the room at my audience and, as I expected, noticed that many of them looked sad and deflated. They needed brightening up. So, instead of beginning my talk with the familiar introduction, I took a deep breath and burst into a loud, rousing verse of 'O Sole Mio'.

Some of my audience jumped with the shock, others started to laugh; more joined in the words, while people randomly started to applaud. However, the single most common effect was that they were now all sitting upright, smiling and laughing, and no longer sad and deflated. The jubilant mood lasted for the rest of the evening, which made my task a lot more enjoyable. So what exactly happened to my audience?

Well, for a start, singing brings joy to people. It is a natural healer. It strengthens the immune system, acts as a workout, and improves your posture. Singing is also a natural antidepressant because it releases endorphins, the feel-good brain chemical that makes you feel joyful and uplifted. Scientists have also identified a tiny organ in the inner region of the ear called the sacculus, which reacts to the frequencies created by singing. This reaction creates a feeling of pleasure almost instantly, regardless of what the singing sounds like.

Singing also lowers stress and anxiety levels and improves mental alertness. Improved blood circulation and an oxygenated bloodstream allow more oxygen to reach the brain. This improves concentration, mental alertness and memory. Towards the end of the evening, much to my surprise, my audience started shouting out for another song before they went home.

A close friend of ours visits her mother in the residential home she has lived in now for some time as a result of Alzheimer's disease. Sadly her mother no longer recognises her or her grandchildren; yet she is able to sing along, word for word, to the songs her daughter has compiled for her on her Spotify app. She doesn't know what a mobile phone is anymore, but she points to it because it's the source of her music, and as soon as her old sixties favourites begin to play, she sings along with them as though she is back there living out her teenage years, much like how Martina Gonzalez reacted to *Swan Lake*.

So what's the big deal about singing? What has singing got to do with chronic illness? The answer is harmony; not the singing variety, but the physiological type that I spoke about earlier, namely homeostasis – or the bodily systems' lack of it. Let me explain.

I function best when all of my bodily systems are performing at a consistent baseline level. My body prefers a core temperature of about 98.6°F (37.0°C), and blood pressure within a manageable range of 90–120 (systolic), over 60–80 (diastolic), according to the American Heart Association. Like clockwork, without ever having to give it any conscious thought, all of the various bodily systems inside me, such as movement, blood pressure, heartbeat, breathing, digestion, swallowing and balance, cooperate and coordinate with each other every second of the day and night to keep my entire body and all its functioning systems in perfect balance. This perfect balance is known as homeostasis.

It's a state of harmony and equilibrium between body and mind. Most of the time, when I find myself in this state, I am not even aware of it. It just *is*. It's more than just feeling content and peaceful. If you have ever experienced that moment when you get a feeling that says, 'everything is just as it should be right now', then you are most likely as close as you will get to being consciously aware of homeostasis.

If you have ever watched the perfectly concentrated poise of a professional opera singer performing on stage, they are most likely in this close-to-perfect state of homeostasis. Singing requires controlled breathing that regulates the heart rate, triggers a relaxation response and brings the body's complex map of systems to a homeostasis that generates feelings of wellbeing. Of course you don't have to be a professional opera singer to experience homeostasis. You can experience it in your own kitchen singing karaoke.

Singing improves your mood, builds your self-esteem, demands that you focus your concentration, and gives you the chance to express difficult emotions. The brief feeling you experience after singing a beautiful song, and hearing the applause of the audience in appreciation of your performance, is homeostasis. Your body is in perfect sync. As a result, you feel a combination of joy, exhilaration, and a pervasive sense of peace and wellbeing. Unfortunately, chronic illness is the great thief of homeostasis.

As I write this, I am into my third year since my diagnosis of MSA. Maybe I should have noticed long before going to the doctor with my list of symptoms that I had stopped singing. This might not be regarded as important when a consultant is charting your medical history during your initial appointment, asking you to think back over a period when you started to notice either subtle or significant changes within your body, and in your daily routine. I don't recall saying to my neurologist, 'I notice that I'm not singing as often as I used to.' A 'reluctance to sing' is not on the list of symptoms that might point to a possibility of my disease, or on the list of symptoms of any other chronic illness, to the best of my knowledge, including cancer. But maybe it should be. Why?

It is very difficult to sing when you are in pain, and your body's systems are out of balance. Even before the pain of an illness manifests itself, the subtle warning signs are there. When a bird stops singing, it's a sign that it is hurt. Singing is a sign of happiness, a sign of harmony; the melody happens almost simultaneously. We may not be aware, but we are in this perfect state of *flow*, a state of complete immersion in an activity, as the American-Hungarian psychologist Mihály Csíkszentmihályi describes it.

Imagine for a moment that you are running a marathon. You have trained hard for it, and the day has arrived. Your attention is focused on every movement of your body, the air in your lungs, the power of your muscles, the sheer strength of your legs, and the feel of the surface you are running on. You are living in the moment, so completely absorbed that you don't notice the time slipping away. You are like a gliding cheetah. This is the mental state of *flow*.

In the movie version of *Les Misérables*, I cry every time I listen to Samantha Barks in her role as Éponine, singing 'On My Own', and Anne Hathaway as Fantine, as she sings 'I Dreamed A Dream'. These are tears of pure joy that I cannot prevent. I am in a state of *flow*; my body is experiencing *homeostasis*. These are perfect moments of harmony within the physiology of the body. But unfortunately these moments are rare and brief. Shortly after experiencing them, we are quickly brought back to reality. The stress and pressure of normal life takes over once again.

As I read back over these pages, I can see that I am adjusting to my new life, thanks to the challenges I have set for myself (including my karaoke challenge) and to my mission statements that make me want more than anything to live my life to its fullest, despite where this illness will take me in the future.

Chapter 20

AN EPIPHANY IN A CAR PARK

It was a warm afternoon during May 2020, and I found myself in a car park. Nothing unusual about that, you might say. The car park had capacity for about two thousand cars, I reckoned, as I stood beside my car looking around at this enormous space, but it was empty except for my car that day. I was waiting to collect a friend. It was during the first coronavirus lockdown. Some of the strict measures imposed on us had been lifted, but those who could continue to work from home were advised to do so.

I had almost an hour to wait before my friend called me to say he was ready to leave work. Normally this car park, with its perfectly allocated, white-painted spaces, would be full. Beyond the car park were fields of green grass and trees; farmland and hills as far as the eye could see. I could have been anywhere on earth, as my mother might say.

My windows were wide open. A gentle, warm breeze blew through the car. The door metal was so hot it felt like it could burn my fingers when I touched it for a brief second. Just then, the strangest thought crossed my mind: is this what it feels like to be dead? Would you be alone somewhere, surrounded by the reminders of a life that you are no longer part of? Everything remains as it is, except that there is no one around. You are being given your final chance to see your world as it used to be when you were once a part of it. Now you are dead. You no longer belong here. The world you once knew so well is empty as you are leaving it. I am hovering between two existences, remembering a lifetime spent keeping up appearances, being seen to do what's right, and tolerating other people's grievances and criticisms. Maybe this is what this empty car park represents once this life is over: all those routines, demands and expectations that you once believed were part of the act of living are no longer a part of wherever it is you find yourself.

I looked across the car park, at the shimmering heat haze in the distance. I wondered how many thousands of men and women had spent their entire working lives parking their cars here in the early mornings and clocking up their hours so they could leave again that evening. Many of them, I am sure, knew that the future had nothing different in store for them, that they would keep doing this day after day until they retired, or became ill, or just grew weary of it and one day never came back. Each of us lives an illusion as we unconsciously move from year to year, working in the hope that the work we do will make a difference, whatever that difference might be. Maybe we are trying to make a better life for our loved ones through the long hours we have no choice in agreeing to do, or maybe we are trying to give a better quality of life to others in another part of the world, or in a location within our own neighbourhood, a quality of life that we might never know we made. But we do it, every day, for hours and hours, because it's our purpose. Until eventually it is no longer our purpose and we are left wondering if there could have been a better purpose. How many of them experienced that emptiness every morning as they drove here and parked their cars?

I asked myself what was the point of my life. Before all this, I entertained people on my radio show. I helped people through my counselling practice. But all that was long gone now.

Perhaps this giant car park represents a sense of freedom for me, now that I am no longer confined to the restrictions of a daily job. It's empty, and vast, and uncluttered. Could this be the mind's way of telling me that this diagnosis has given me greater space within my life to explore what is important to me in the time I have left here? I can juggle my life of normality with this new more 'spacious' chapter – one that urges me to explore, and to find space, like an empty beach, or a rambling forest path. There are many nights when I sit outside the patio door and stare up into the sky. I love the clear, frosty nights because I can instantly pick out those familiar constellations that I learned about as a young boy that keep me forever young because they never change. Stars and planets and suns like speckled dots in the huge vastness of space. The beauty of the clear night sky gives me that sense of freedom that comes with space. No illness can ever be a match for the power of the universe. That thought gives me peace from the fear of what lies ahead.

I love writing. It allows me to step through a door where I can find freedom on a blank screen. I love books so much that I feel at home when I am surrounded by them. I love the prospect of visiting a bookshop. It's not like any other shop because it has a timeless resonance about it. Time stands still. Booksellers are a different breed. Many of them gladly give themselves over to their bookshops. And they are not just shops: they are studios, workshops and meeting places, where they'll make you a coffee and suggest where to browse. Their belonging is also their purpose. They are energised by the beautiful smell that comes from a brand new page of writing that is opened for the very first time. There is a sense of belonging in spending time browsing through books new and old, and then eavesdropping on choices that other browsers are considering as they take books down from the shelves.

Maybe I am depressed, I think to myself. 'Depressed.' I say it out loud. Then I shout it at the top of my voice. No one can hear me. I remember a woman telling me that for months after her husband died she would visit a park early each morning when no one else was there, and she would kneel on the grass and scream out her husband's name until her voice became hoarse. He never answered. 'Does that mean he can't hear me?' she asked me. 'Or is it because there is nothing left of him?'

Her questions have stayed with me for over twenty years. When I die, will I still be able to hear people I loved talking about me? Or will there be nothing left of me, except the air that I once breathed?

One of the first books I read on depression was by the psychologist Dorothy Rowe. It was called *Depression: The Way Out of Your Prison*. It is a powerful book in which Rowe talks about how important it is to reach an understanding of ourselves in order to gain an insight into depression. I could quote from every page because her words left such an impression on me. Rowe also explains that it is through awareness of our mortality that our ongoing life discovers its purpose. Life has to be significant to each of us, even if it can't be, or appears not to be, to other people. Accepting the knowledge of our death sets us free to live fully. It's often only when we become ill that we finally set out on a journey to get to know ourselves. In order to start that journey we need to unclutter our lives. Maybe that's what the significance of the empty car park was for me that day: I was uncluttering my life and finding the space I needed to explore – new space, new life, new freedom.

I often wonder if my life has become less significant because I no longer do the job I loved doing. But that would be to give it all the credit for making my life worthwhile, and of course that is not true. I feel very fortunate to have done something I loved so much and to have got paid for it. I know I never wanted it to end during those years when I was in that state of flow during each radio show, but the human mind constantly needs to be challenged. It needs a full 'mind makeover' every few years, otherwise it gets bored and life becomes predictable.

Chronic illness wreaks havoc on families and friendships, among other things. Its cruel destruction hurts fragile relationships that haven't had a chance to heal. Life-threatening illness very often becomes the elephant in the room that some family members can't discuss, or face up to, or accept in others whom they love. They can't bear to be around suffering that is too close for comfort, or to acknowledge that creeping uncertainty about what lies ahead. So instead, some people choose to keep their distance, and slowly that distance becomes greater over the weeks and months, sometimes years. It becomes a door many people can't walk back through because they are afraid of what will confront them on the far side, and what the consequences will mean for them. For some, it can often feel too painful to reach out, to roll up their sleeves and muck in with the uncomfortable tasks associated with looking after a loved one who is slowly dying. Others silently believe that if they avoid the messiness of another's chronic illness, they will be spared the equally messy period of grieving that person when they're gone. Out of sight, out of mind. But that's not the way it works – neither in sickness, nor in death.

Illness can be such an inconvenience for others, whose own lives are forced to change because of the illness that is slowly changing the life of the person they love. They'll never admit to it, but it's there. Many people with chronic illness have told me they are only too aware of this form of silent conflict, possibly the harshest of all rejections. Such a sense of 'angry' inconvenience is more prevalent than we might think.

As a result of my own illness, I have forged lasting connections and friendships with people who are on their own lonely paths due to life-threatening conditions. I'm disheartened at how many of them have family members or friends who show no interest in supporting them during these poignant stages of a life in decline. Sadly, for some who turn their back on the plight of others, it's a way of removing themselves from their responsibility to the sick individual because of something they may have done in the past; while for others, such chronic illness is merely an inconvenience in their busy life, and they choose distraction as the best way of avoiding a troubled conscience.

Chronic illness is often a heart-breaking journey. It doesn't have to be that way, but can be made more emotionally cruel by the seemingly wilful decisions of others not to share the intimacy of the final journey – until sadly the inevitable happens, and the chance to reach out is gone forever. To all those who find themselves in that place, I genuinely hope you find a new belonging.

My thoughts and awareness had shifted now. I saw this car park as a great big empty space that needed to be filled with the rest of my life. This was like so many car parks I had used over the years when my routine was busy and I never had enough time to catch up. But those days were gone. I had all the space in the world.

Maintaining an inner resistance to being pushed aside by this illness was the most important thing now.

When you receive bad news involving your health, the present becomes a terrifying place. You become frozen in time. We wake each morning thinking of all the bad stuff that lies ahead of us. I often have to remind myself that my entire future is beyond my personal control, and I am only wasting precious time by being afraid of it. Those of us with chronic illness don't wake up and think about how we're going to embrace that morning, or what plans we might make for the evening. We become consumed with the bleak emptiness of a future that is uncertain and possibly difficult and painful, and we waste those precious moments when we find ourselves in empty spaces that we can choose to fill in whatever way we want to.

Death is out there somewhere. Once we can find an inner peace and accept that fact, we can find these empty spaces deep within us and fill them with something that gives our life purpose, if not for ourselves, then for others. Renaissance philosopher Michel de Montaigne once said, 'If you fear suffering, then you are already suffering from what you fear.'

Shortly after my diagnosis, an elderly woman called Mona who lived close to my apartment squeezed my hand one afternoon when we met in our local newsagent's. She told me she would light a candle for my intentions at mass the next morning. I met Mona again the following week. She told me she had lit a special candle for me every morning since then. 'Bad things happen to good people,' she whispered to me as she held my hands tightly in hers, 'but God will never forsake you in your moments of suffering.' Her faith was as strong as her grip, and I believed her.

'Do you mind if I ask you a question, Mona?'

She seemed delighted with the opportunity to continue the conversation. I sensed she spent most of her days alone. 'Anything you like,' she replied.

'When you talk about God, what do you mean?' I asked.

She thought for a moment and smiled. 'When I talk about God, I sense someone who is more than just a person like you or me; more like someone who allows me to be who I am, but is quick to remind me whenever I am not being true to myself. I feel his presence within me. It's like a belonging that won't leave me stray too far.'

A shiver ran up my spine. For the briefest moment I believed I was looking at Sister Rachel, the nun I had known from the enclosed order during my seminary days. I could have sworn it was her.

I found Mona's words to be so comforting and reassuring that I took out my notebook and wrote them out so I would never forget them. I believe that each of us is sent people like Mona at times in our lives when we most need to be reminded that we are not alone, even though the loneliness we are feeling can be so inwardly destructive that we feel like giving up.

Paula lights a small candle on the windowsill in our kitchen first thing every morning. It is one of the most beautiful gestures I have ever witnessed. The white candle nestles below a sculpted wooden statue of the Holy Family, a reflection of a family whose welcome is based on inclusiveness and not segregation. Then she takes a photo of the candle flame and uploads it to her Facebook page with the caption, 'especially for anyone who needs this today'. The replies come instantly.

We all need to be reminded that we belong to something much greater and more inclusive than what we might have to settle for in our daily lives; and what better way to be drawn into the presence that is within each of us than by a beautiful, selfless gesture that sends out hope to someone who might just need it at that very moment.

Too often we imagine a God who exists outside of us, somewhere high up there in the heavens. Whenever we think of loved ones who have died, we imagine that they are 'up above' watching over us, and they in turn are closer to the God we pray to so that he will continue to mind us as we walk this journey without them.

If there is one certainty about receiving a diagnosis of a chronic, incurable illness, it's this: you will think long and hard about the real meaning of life; by real, I mean what is true and supportive to you. It is usually at some point after receiving such bad news that each of us believes that life has always been solitary, but that we have managed admirably to block out the solitude and temporarily fill the space with our never-ending drive to 'live the dream'; to have everything we have always desired.

Most people stay focused on living within their comfort zone, but dream of being wild and spontaneous, and stepping outside that comfort zone into the unknown. I mentioned earlier that there is hope in the unknown, which is why most people wish they had the courage to explore the unknown. I'm not talking about retracing the footsteps of Antarctic explorer Tom Crean on his *Terra Nova* Expedition. I am talking about the 'unknown' that exists within each and every one of us. Within this unknown region lies the answer to the age-old question: Who am I?

Perhaps my experience in the empty car park that afternoon was my psyche's way of reminding me that I have found a new and enriching freedom. Maybe it was telling me that finding a space I can fit into every day of the week is not what my life is about anymore. The space I once fit into is no longer important to me, and I no longer have to keep looking for it. It's the time that has been freed up by removing me from that old space that is my focus now, and what to do with this time so that it will help to make a difference in the lives of others who are also searching.

Chapter 21

GOING BACK TO MY ROOTS

One recent Saturday, under a mackerel sky of diffused bronze and orange ripples slowly giving way to a crystal-clear azure dawn, Paula and I set out in the car on a journey that I had been planning to make for many years. We were stepping back in time, back into another world. It would be a journey into the unknown, which would afford us a glimpse of my ancestors that I knew very little about, but about whom I now needed to know as much as I possibly could.

Maybe this is a common psychological phenomenon that happens when you find out that the unconscious free-flow of life on autopilot has hit a wall, like when your car gets a puncture and you have to pull in and figure out how to change a wheel before you can go any further. You try to remember the last time you jacked up the car and unbolted a wheel. It's probably years since you did it. Once the wheel is changed, you move on; but your journey feels different now. You're no longer free-wheeling. You're slightly nervous and distracted. The road ahead takes on a new, more cautious perspective because now you know you don't have a spare wheel at your disposal anymore so you can't afford to risk another puncture. For the rest of the journey you can't really relax because all the wonderful plans you have made are put on hold until you find a garage where you can get the punctured tyre patched up again. Instead of letting life just carry you along almost aimlessly, you imagine breaking down in the middle of nowhere, where the roads are empty and phone coverage is nil, and crossroads no longer have signposts.

This was how my life felt for a long time after my neurologist added some letters after my name that I never asked for, *Gareth O'Callaghan MSA*. No matter how free I tried to feel, there was a prohibitive effect that came with the diagnosis, a destiny I had no control over. My present was a place I was still becoming accustomed to and didn't like, and my future was a product of my vivid imagination, and it scared me. What lay ahead made me anxious, so what better way to avoid the misplaced fear of any future preconceived notions than to go back in time to explore the beautiful hinterlands where my ancestors had grown up.

I once asked my good friend John O'Donohue, 'Where do we go when we die?' We had met briefly for coffee and a chat some years back, shortly after he had written *Eternal Echoes: Celtic Reflections on Our Yearning to Belong*, and he was preparing to return to America for a book tour and some speaking engagements. John thought carefully for a moment, and then replied, 'Nowhere! There *is* nowhere to go when we die. We just stay *here.* It makes perfect sense to me now. John is long gone, sadly, but his spirit and his presence infuse many of the wonderful places in the west of Ireland where he always returned to over the years in order to immerse himself in the landscape that was at the very root of his writings.

I always thought that John O'Donohue exuded an other-worldly quality in the many ways he spoke about the beauty of the divine. God is all around us, just like those we love who have died and 'crossed over'. They stay close to us. That is my belief. I have encountered many people during my life who have exuded similar compassion in the transcendent, almost superhuman ways in which they live their lives; being in their presence, even at a distance, has always had a profound effect on me. These people are not famous – I have met them on the bus, in my local supermarket, handing out dinners in a local hostel, holding the hand of someone who is spending their final hours in the care of a hospice, praying quietly in a solitary pew in an empty church on a winter's afternoon when it just felt good for me to veer off my path and sit, occasionally watching their prayers being sent off to those in need. I love to sit towards the back of these places of worship, in the silence of the ancients, for half an hour while I contemplate another side of life – one that includes God; or maybe I just sit there and ask God to send me a sign. I am in no doubt that there is a universal force of power and good that is not just central to my life, but also to the world and to the greater universe that I live in. Even the majority of doctors, according to recent surveys, say they believe in 'some type of God'. In February 1954, just fourteen months before he died, Albert Einstein wrote a letter to the American physicist David Bohm. In it he said, 'If God created the world, his primary concern was certainly not to make its understanding easy for us.' Meanwhile, in the famous words of David Bohm, 'In the long run it is far more dangerous to adhere to illusion than to face what the actual fact is.'

Do I pray? Yes I do. I think I am constantly praying, but not usually in the traditional form where I kneel in a church and direct my attention towards a crucifix suspended over an altar. That said, I did exactly that last week in my local church here in Cork. I asked for strength to write this very piece that I am typing right now. I asked my higher power to guide me with the most appropriate words that might convey to my readers exactly how I feel about God, considering I didn't want to offend the readers' feelings. I am aware that everybody has a different take on God; that's perfectly fine. If we all had identical beliefs, then God wouldn't make for such an interesting conversational topic. Mostly I walk and talk to my God, connecting with that sense of spirit that I feel around me as a central part of my life. God is very real, but to regard him, or refer to him, as 'he' (or even as 'she') is to simplify the magnificence of all that comes from nature and the universe.

David Bohm believed that each of us is fundamentally connected to all other beings and in contact with the *plenum*, which means spiritual being. Panendeism, a fairly recently coined term which probably comes close to my own beliefs, is the belief in a God who contains the whole universe but who is also bigger than the universe. Panendeists believe in a god that is present in everything but extends beyond the universe. This would infer that God is the universe but is also greater than the universe. Can I form a relationship with this God? Of course I can because this God is everywhere, in everything. Is this a description of my God? I think it must be, because it's impossible to describe in a few carefully selected words what my God is; that would only undermine the omnipotent, pervasive presence of this universal power.

Those who are blessed to grow up surrounded by the beauty of nature have no desire to stray too far from the landscape they belong to, because if they do, part of their purpose is lost. It's constantly calling them back. If they must leave for a while, they make it their business to return. Depression cannot exist when a human life is infused with the spirit of nature, because depression is really just the painful longing of the neglected soul; and no soul is ever neglected while it is embraced by the freedom of nature, a freedom that it belongs within, which it can't survive without, and which eventually calls it back home forever.

This was my reason to go out and find these places. My ancestors might have left the physical world behind them hundreds of years ago, but their spirits, free to roam forever, still permeate this beautiful countryside. Time is a commodity that doesn't interest nature. Nature is its own world, and can only be truly experienced when time is set aside. Architectural designs might represent the culmination of years of hard work by masterful minds who believe they have created a work of art and beauty. But such works pale in comparison to a monarch butterfly you hold carefully on the back of your hand for the briefest moment as you study its intricate, natural beauty that defies human logic. To embrace nature is to fully embrace freedom, and that is why nature in all its beauty, I believe, nurtures the human spirit throughout its natural life and welcomes it back home at the end of its journey. Nature heals us because nature owns us.

My mother had often shown me grainy black-and-white photographs of family groups and relations of hers. Both of her parents were from Cork, and the lineage of both families stretches back as far as official records go, to include hinterlands and place names like Aghabullogue, Mullinhassig, Aghinagh, Carrigadrohid, Berrings, and a tiny little crossroads village in the hinterland of Gortdonaghmore called Matehy.

These were all places that I associate with my childhood, when we would spend long stretches of our summer holidays – having debunked from the noisy bustle of Dublin city in exchange for the feeling of complete freedom around these parts – wading in the shallow, rockier stretches of the River Shornaugh, which flows down from the Boggeragh mountains to join the River Lee by Carrigrohane, picking up the Blarney and Martin rivers along its route.

Why was I doing this? For years my brother, my late father and my cousin Susan had been chipping away at family trees, searching back through troves of historical information and locating names and places none of us were really familiar with. Now I lived in Cork city, barely half an hour's drive from these townlands and historic family origins that extended back hundreds of years, long before official records were kept. Illiteracy was a huge problem for so many generations, which no doubt explains why little is known about most families before a certain point in time. For most of us, all that exists is what was written into the census form that was updated every four years, as it continues to be.

My interest initially was fired up when I discovered the name of a Garret Callahan from Coachford, who existed as part of my mother's very distant family way back in the late 1700s. Maybe now that I was accepting the inevitability of mortality, it seemed reasonable to want to know more about those lives that were interconnected to mine through long-forgotten generations. We all eventually become forgotten after we die. That just didn't seem fair to me. Of course I probably wouldn't have been thinking that way if I hadn't received the news that my own life was now in the balance.

Part of accepting our mortality is to appreciate that those who have gone before us still have a spiritual connection to us. Unhindered by time and space, they reach out to us in a way that tells me they are as alive now in spirit as they were when they walked the narrow, winding roads of these beautifully named townlands. Their lives here may have long ended, but their presence lives on and continues its resonance within us. Each of us is naturally drawn to the past, since that is where we have lived out most of our lives so far. All that we have done is behind us, even though it has moulded each of us into what we are today.

We had planned it for a dry day, as we reckoned there could be some hiking involved. We had packed strong walking boots and the customary rainwear, along with a small lunch we had prepared the night before in the event that most likely there wouldn't be any grocery pit stops along the way.

We turned off the normally hectic N40 west, and within minutes we were driving along the most beautiful country roads, with rich, mature trees on either side that leaned over and reached out to each other, forming the most perfect green arch. It struck me that some of these trees were over one hundred years old, with many of the walls and deserted ruins stretching back through generations long gone. I got a sense of what it must have been like to live in this unspoilt part of the world many generations ago.

Our journey that day was the culmination of months of research. I was trying to locate the grave of my great-grandparents. I have always loved strolling around ancient rural graveyards, sitting for hours beside gravestones that have been eroded by hundreds of years of harsh weather, trying to identify family names, ages and townlands, while attempting to tie in dates of death with past wars and famine times. The siblings and the grandchildren who might once have cared for the dilapidated, overgrown graves of those buried here are not just gone themselves now but also long forgotten. I am reminded that long after I am gone, there will come a time when everyone who ever knew me will also be forgotten.

All I knew was that their remains were buried in one of the oldest cemeteries in County Cork, close to Blarney, in the picturesque hinterland of Matehy, where a tiny, overgrown graveyard sits opposite a small, beautiful Catholic church called St James's. The locals were neighbourly and welcoming, and quick to inform us that few if any visitors to this most historic location pronounce Matehy correctly. Its correct pronunciation is 'maw-te-ha', which might be translated as the 'Plain of the Retreat' – as in the sense of fleeing. Matehy consists of a small cluster of houses, a fine school, a pub called 'The Strand Bar', a small, disused post office, a garage for tractor repairs, and this most imposing graveyard. It's a sleepy hamlet that, if it weren't for the growing number of luxury houses being constructed in the area, could be described as existing on the edge of time itself.

From the moment we parked the car next to the church, I fell in love with the place. Was that because two people who were partly responsible for my birth had left their mortal bones behind them here when their time came to depart this life? Perhaps it all comes back to Jung's theory of the 'collective unconsciousness', which he described as 'a second psychic system of a collective, universal and impersonal nature which is identifiable in all individuals'. Every single human being is permanently connected to this stream of collective unconscious thoughts, which, Jung says, 'comprises in itself the psychic life of our ancestors, right back to the earliest beginnings'.

I firmly believe that if we leave our minds open, unbiased and welcoming, we quickly find ourselves thinking in a completely different way. That is because we are now tuned in to the infinite collective unconsciousness. How many times have you been trying to remember a name, perhaps for days, only to suddenly recall it when you weren't even focusing on it? Have you ever found yourself in that situation where you decide at the last second not to drive through the amber light at a traffic intersection, only to realise in a fraction of a second that a car coming in the other direction has broken the red light and would have hit you side-on if you had crossed the junction?

Children up to the age of three are almost permanently tuned in to this infinite collective unconsciousness. It's why they talk to their 'imaginary friends' – as parents and teachers call them. Except they're far from imaginary; their tiny brains are like sponges, soaking up the thoughts and the sounds of the invisible unconsciousness that floats through their unaffected minds. They are naturally tapping into previous generations of spiritual energy and chat that they relate to by talking back to it. Just as each of us did when we were their age – but then we grew up.

It can also happen when a critically ill person has reached the end stage of life. They might have been in a coma for days, when all of a sudden they become animated, and open their eyes. They seem to be looking beyond you as they mumble words as if they're focusing on a person in the room that no one else can see. They might even try to sit up in the bed, and reach for something, or someone.

Doctors often put this down to the high doses of morphine and sedatives; but once you begin to understand the stream of infinite collective unconsciousness, you realise that as their mind becomes less agitated and confused, as they get closer to death and their systems are tiring, they are focusing now on very little; so their minds are free to slip into the stream of invisible unconsciousness, where they tap into the energy and the thinking of those who have gone before them.

This happened to my grandmother shortly before she died. She had been living with us since she'd had a bad stroke, which had left her bedridden. Late one night as I quietly climbed the stairs after coming in late from work, I could hear her voice. She was speaking to someone. It was after two in the morning and the rest of the household was fast asleep, so she wasn't chatting with my mother.

As I reached the top of the stairs, a brilliant orange

light outlined her closed bedroom door. It wasn't like the normal nightstand light that she kept on during the night, as it seemed to fluctuate in brightness. My gran was chatting, as if answering questions from the source of the light. As I gently turned the handle and eased open the door, the light suddenly vanished and the room was now dark again. The light from the landing lit up the room enough for me to make out her face in the bed. Her eyes were open and she was smiling at me. I could feel a shiver run down my spine, but not in a frightening way. I knew she had been talking to my grandad who had died six years before. It was as though he had come to collect her and bring her home. She passed away shortly after that night.

We left Matehy two hours later, having found my great-grandparents' grave. It was a very moving experience, standing there together in the beautiful afternoon sunshine, in the perfect silence of this hallowed place that earlier generations might have affectionately known as God's acre. As we stood in quiet reflection looking down at this piece of ground that showed no signs of a final resting place except for the white granite boulder that marked it, I wondered what they both looked like, what their daily routines must have consisted of. These were people who survived the Spanish Flu of 1918 and the years that followed. If they had succumbed to it, like tens of thousands did here in Ireland, then I wouldn't be writing this.

So many of the gravestones had deteriorated to the point where they were just circular mounds of granite in the ground. We searched the ancient, hallowed grounds, stumbling on graves that dated back to the late 1700s. But the names and the dates were gone on all but a few upright headstones. We enjoyed our short visit that day, but it served yet again as a reminder to me that our time here is so brief. And once again, on our short journey back home, I could feel that familiar sense of vulnerability. I am determined to live as long and as full a life as I possibly can. If a cure for this illness comes along, then so be it; but I'm not going to hang around waiting for it to happen. I have too much living left to do.

When we die, our bodies return to the earth; yet it's from that same earth that all of nature's greatest beauty emerges and life once again thrives. Death is the end of life as we know it, but each of us lives on in the beauty of nature that we will all someday return to. I believe that part of the next life involves us becoming the spirit in nature. We are reborn into the beauty of nature that surrounds us, and in that beauty we get to live forever. Surely that is an exciting prospect.

Think of the cool breeze of autumn as it brushes your cheek with an almost familiar scent that makes you smile, the sunshine on your face on a summer's day that for a brief moment gives you a familiar sense of the belonging that connects us all infinitely, or the tiny robin redbreast that sits on your kitchen windowsill reminding you of someone you miss, whose spirit connects to yours through the beauty and mystery of such a tiny, vulnerable creature. And for the briefest of moments, time stands still; you are reminded that life and nature can never be separated.

And Finally
For Now...

It was on a gloriously sunny September afternoon in 2020, complete with those magnificent high, blue skies, when the two of us left home in a beautiful Audi A6 sporting the slick gunmetal colour that Paula has always loved. We arrived at the registry office fifteen minutes before our appointed time of three o'clock. Only weeks before, the government had re-introduced the COVID-19 restrictions due to an unfortunate increase in confirmed cases. So far there was not going to be a complete shutdown similar to what we all had to endure the previous March, but our suspicions remained that it wasn't too far away. The thought that our wedding would once again be postponed indefinitely was just too much to bear. Thankfully this time it was going ahead. Our small party huddled in the hallway, all wearing protective masks. Paula looked stunning in a blush pink retro-style dress and pink sparkly shoes. I was wearing a suit for the first time in years, and I felt good, very good.

Grooms are rarely remembered for what they wear at their own weddings. That honour goes to the bride, and rightfully so. Paula looked beautiful and so happy as she stood opposite me and we exchanged our vows. She was glowing. We held hands for most of the twenty-minute ceremony. It was the culmination of five very long and uncertain years, during which time we had received news of a diagnosis that we expected would change our lives forever. I never once doubted that we would marry each other, but I was fearful of what lay ahead, considering that Paula would eventually become my fulltime carer if this illness finally progressed to that stage. But that afternoon, just like on so many other afternoons, I was adamant that I was going to beat this illness, just to prove to those who told me I couldn't, that I could. And I will go on fighting it for the rest of my life.

Our registrar declared us married, and those who had gathered with us to celebrate this all-time special moment clapped and cheered. Carol, Paula's sister, watched the ceremony live on FaceTime from her home in Buckingham, in England. She should have been Paula's matron of honour that day, but couldn't travel because of the health restrictions. It was a day that will shine brightly in our hearts forever. In the days that followed, due to what appeared would be a further escalation of COVID-19 restrictions surrounding social gatherings, which by then seemed inevitable, we discussed the possibility that we may have to postpone a larger celebration that we had planned for our extended families and friends in October. The waiting game had started once again.

I hope, and firmly believe, that in another book I will be able to continue the detail and finally complete this love story that had begun unexpectedly in that 'sliding doors' moment one March night six years ago in a nightclub in Cork.

As these final words find their place here, I am already planning my next writing excursion. I have no idea where it might take me, but that's the exciting challenge that comes with writing about feelings and fears, hopes and dreams, and love and laughter. Before I sign off for now, there is still one piece of the jigsaw that deserves a mention. In fact, maybe it deserves its own book when I consider how important it has become in maintaining my inner wellbeing, sustaining my hope, and in restoring my resilience: that is nature.

Recently during a visit to Dublin for a medical appointment I visited the Phoenix Park very early that morning before heading to the clinic. This beautiful nature reserve is just a stone's throw from where I grew up. I have lost count of all the times I went there over the years when my life was balancing on a cliff edge, and I always found the peace that I had come looking for. I found this healing peace in nature, and still do; I know now I always will. Over these past three challenging years, nature is what I keep coming back to because it's the source of my hope and resilience.

Nature is my true spiritual home; it's not just mine, it's everyone's.

I had been watching a small herd of deer grazing on the wide-open expanses of grass. The morning was barely bright, and I had inched my way as close to them as I could without disturbing them. The slightest noise, and they would be gone. They were aware of me but they didn't seem bothered by my presence. Just for the briefest moment I felt as though they had accepted me into their world. It was a simple place, from what I could gather, a world where courage and resilience and belonging was what they knew. They weren't interested in the hectic city life and the non-stop noise that existed just beyond the walls of this gentle preserve. Their sense of freedom was what mattered to them, and also their sense of belonging. Theirs was not a world of exclusion. For that briefest moment I felt as though I was allowed to share their quiet space. It's moments like these that have helped me to get through the last few years.

Behind them was the forest where I love to walk at every opportunity, with its permanent inhabitants – oak, ash, sycamore, beech, lime and horse-chestnut

– many of them growing tall long before I was born. It's as though the trees invite me into their world. I'm never in a hurry to leave beautiful forests such as this because they remind me of my unbreakable bond with nature. Nature is where we belong; it's our natural habitat. Too many of us have lost that connection with nature; I genuinely believe it's possibly one of the biggest reasons why chronic illness is more common in recent years.

I think I have adjusted to my diagnosis now, almost three years after receiving it. Maybe the extra space that I have in my life these days makes me realise that time spent in nature is as important to the human mind and body as the quality of the food we eat. Trees inspire me, in a way that very few humans could ever do. It takes twenty-two trees to produce enough oxygen to keep one human being healthy and happy. Without trees, our entire existence would crumble. Trees keep us alive. That's a fact. They help us to feel less anxious and more restored. 'Forest bathing', as it has become known, is time spent among trees. It works wonders for your mental health. Nature restores the neglected soul. It breathes new life into the spirit of who we are. Lately I have been telling anyone who will listen, that each of us needs to go back to spending quality time in nature. That is how we will each find a way out of our darkness. Covid-19 has left so many people spiritually homeless and emotionally wrecked. That might have included me, if I hadn't received such bad health news back in 2018. That was what left me spiritually homeless; so when Covid-19 came along early last year, I guess I was already in search of a new spiritual home. Thankfully I found it, and the good news is that it's timeless.

It's important in these times of illness and loss to remind ourselves that the spirit within each of us is timeless. Those we mourn and miss are closer than we know. The life that others see in us is not the life we live. No one can see that life, and that's how it should be. It's up to each of us to live a life where freedom and belonging join together at the heart of everything we do, and to cultivate a rich inner life filled with courage and resilience, with hope at its core. It's also up to each of us to do it before it's too late. The starting point for me, and I still do it every chance I get, was a spot of 'forest bathing.'

As I set out now on the next stage of my journey, I focus on the positive impressions, maybe formed without conscious thought or on the basis of little evidence; I am no longer afraid of whatever lies ahead of me. This is my life, so I want to be the one who decides how it will be best spent. This should also be your motto, if you find yourself in a similar predicament. Life is all about loving, and feeling loved, and reaching out, and giving back, even if that is just for a short time longer. There can be no other legacy more important.

This illness leaves me feeling very vulnerable in the face of what I'm told is inevitable; but within that vulnerability, where there is no room for deferral, complacency or resignation, lies courage. It's easy to stand with the crowd; it takes courage to stand alone, like one of those wise old trees that reminds me to stand tall, straighten up, push my shoulders back, and breathe in deeply the healing benefits of nature.

It's only through the seeds of courage that I can nurture the resilience – the bounce-back-ability factor – that I need to keep living a full and meaningful life. That's the challenge that lies ahead of me. That's what matters now. I've heard it said by people who have been diagnosed with chronic illness that we simplify our lives in order to endear ourselves to the untold time we have left here. And the length of that time is no longer important because we have already set ourselves free.

Further Reading

What Matters Now has taken me over two years to complete. I have always had a passion for writing. It's the same for reading. If I were to add up the hours in my life that I have spent browsing in traditional bookshops, I have no doubt it would stretch to months. I never leave a bookshop without buying a book. I have included a list of titles here that you might be interested in. While some of the titles reflect upon themes I have written about, many of them are simply wonderful books that I have enjoyed, in recent times and in the past. I hope you enjoy them too.

Elman, Dave, *Hypnotherapy* (Westwood Publishing, 1964)

Erickson, Milton H., *My Voice Will Go with You* (W.W. Norton & Company, 1991)

Fox, Michael J., *No Time Like the Future* (Headline, 2020)

Francis, Paul, *The Shamanic Journey: A Practical Guide to Therapeutic Shamanism* (Paul Francis, 2017)

Frankl, Viktor E., *Man's Search for Meaning* (Ebury Publishing, 2011)

Fredrickson, Renee, *Repressed Memories: A Journey to Recovery from Sexual Abuse* (Touchstone, 1992)

Gawande, Atul, *Being Mortal: Illness, Medicine, and What Matters in the End* (Profile Books, 2015)

Graff, Garrett M., *The Only Plane in the Sky: The Oral History of 9/11* (Monoray, 2019)

Groff, Christina, *The Thirst for Wholeness: Attachment, Addiction, and the Spiritual Path* (Harper One, 1994)

Harding, Michael, *What Is Beautiful in the Sky* (Hachette Books Ireland, 2020)

Hoffman, Eva, *Time* (Picador, 2009)

Kalanithi, Paul, *When Breath Becomes Air* (Vintage, 2017)

Keenan, Brian, *An Evil Cradling* (Vintage, 1992)

Keenan, Brian, *Four Quarters of Light: An Alaskan Journey* (Black Swan, 2005)

Kübler-Ross, Elisabeth, *On Death and Dying* (Simon & Schuster, 1969)

May, Gerald G., *The Wisdom of Wilderness: Experiencing the Healing Power of Nature* (Harper One, 2006)

McGillicuddy, Mary, *John Moriarty: Not the Whole Story* (The Lilliput Press, 2018)

Moore, Thomas, *Care of the Soul* (Harper Perennial, 1994)

Obama, Barack, *A Promised Land* (Viking, 2020)

O'Donohue, John, *Anam Cara* (Bantam Books, 1999)

O'Donohue, John, *Eternal Echoes: Celtic Reflections on Our Yearning to Belong* (Bantam Books, 2000)

Poole, Raymond, *Nothing's So Bad That It Couldn't Be Worse* (Book Hub Publishing, 2020)

Richo, David, *The Five Things We Cannot Change…* (Shambhala Publications, 2006)

Rogers, Carl R., *A Way of Being* (Houghton Mifflin Company, 1980)

Rowe, Dorothy, *Depression: The Way Out of Your Prison* (Routledge, 1996)

Ryan, Donal, *From a Low and Quiet Sea* (Black Swan Ireland, 2019)

Scally, John, *Inspiration for All Seasons: Celtic Wisdom for Today* (Black & White, 2020)

Servan-Schreiber, David, MD, PhD, *The Instinct to Heal* (Rodale, 2004)

Siegel, Bernie, *Love, Medicine and Miracles* (Ebury Press, 1999)

Storr, Anthony, *Solitude: A Return to the Self* (The Free Press, 1988)

Storr, Anthony, *The Art of Psychotherapy*, 2nd edn (Routledge, 1990)

Walchars, John, *The Unfinished Mystery* (The Seabury Press, 1978)

Yalom, Irvin D., *Becoming Myself: A Psychiatrist's Memoir* (Piatkus, 2017)

Acknowledgements

Each of us will be affected in some way by serious illness during our lives – whether that's directly, or where you have to watch someone you love suffer the pain and uncertainty of a life-threatening condition. Thanking those who support us during these unexpected times is so important. If I were to even try to acknowledge every individual whose support means so much, then someone would inadvertently be left out. Therefore it's best just to say a sincere thank you. *Semper grata*, as my Latin teacher would say. My life is eternally enriched by your kindness, for knowing you are there. However, it would be remiss of me not to mention those who have played a hands-on role in recent times:

To our extended families and friends, both Paula's and mine, thank you for all your support.

A very special thank you to my editor Ciara Doorley, for not only helping me to bring this idea to life, but for her tireless support as I explored a number of difficult themes here; my gratitude also to Susan Feldstein, whose editorial input made an enormous difference during those more doubtful moments, and whose conversations always gave me food for thought; and special thanks to my team at Hachette Ireland, to Breda Purdue, Jim Binchy, Elaine Egan, Joanna Smyth, Bernard Hoban and Ruth Shern.

My thanks to Sheila Crowley for believing in this book at the very start, long before it would take shape, and for helping it to fly.

My sincere gratitude must go to Suzanne McDonnell for her legal guidance, and her patient, calming encouragement, when the hurdles seemed almost impossible. I wish to thank Willie and Margaret Swaine for their business skills and lasting friendship down through the years. I am also grateful to Gerald Kean, a genuine friend whose gentle tenets of life and steely insights eased me through some formidable challenges.

Ray O'Toole is never far from my thoughts. Ray has been through the wars with his own health issues over the past few years. Despite his own challenges, he continues, with the love and support of his wonderful wife Fiona, to reach out in a way that makes those who know him understand and appreciate true friendship.

I was deeply honoured to be asked by my dear friend John Scally to write the Foreword to his powerful book, *Inspiration for All Seasons: Celtic Wisdom for Today*. John's interest in Celtic spirituality has deeply enriched many lives, including mine. John is certainly one of life's most thoughtful givers. We met some years back and my spirit has been richer for his presence in my life. *Destitutus ventis, remos adhibe.*

Special thanks to Pat Egan, and his beautiful wife Helena. Pat was cool when I was at school. All these years later, he is undoubtedly our 'coolest' friend, and one of Irish music's greatest legends, with an obliging kindness that we will never forget.

I'm sure there are very few people, if any, who manage to navigate the often stormy seas of their own health challenges without the expertise of a good doctor. I'm fortunate that I have a very good one. I am grateful with a thirty-year thank you to Michael Hayes, for his diligent care, his warmth, and his wit.

I will be forever grateful to Seamus Whitney, whom I don't get to see very often these days but whose friendship and long-distance encouragement keeps me moving in the right direction. Seamus and his team of counsellors do marvellous work at Slí Sophia in Kiltegan, County Wicklow.

I am so proud of Daithi O'Connor, and the team at Revive Active in Galway, whenever I am reminded of their amazing achievements and well-deserved awards. I am grateful to you all for your care and consideration over these past few years; and to another lifelong friend, Geoff Canavan, a man gifted with a calming influence, and a positive energy that always lifts me just when I need it most.

I also include here friends I have made as a result of my diagnosis, friends who are also grappling with the huge challenges of life-changing illness. They eat resilience for breakfast. I send heartfelt thanks, and strength for the road ahead, to Kevin Quaid and his wife Helena, Raymond Poole, Gary Boyle, John Wall, and Leo Forde.

No matter how difficult the bad days get, the good days always push them aside; and these are the days we will cherish forever and be grateful to those who made them happen. I am thinking of two good friends: Eoin Daly and his team at The Address Hotel, Cork for the magic they created on our special day, and Neven Maguire and his team for making us feel so special when we visited MacNean House and Restaurant, in County Cavan.

A special word of thanks to all my radio listeners down through the years, across the many radio stations it's been my pleasure to work on, and also to those who follow me on Facebook and Twitter.

There was great sadness last November when Michael Johnston, a fellow MSA warrior and friend, passed away unexpectedly but peacefully. Michael's loss is immense for his family, and I will be forever grateful for the kindness shown to me by them in the midst of their grief. Another dear friend was Bill Brennan, also diagnosed with MSA. Bill was taken from us all too soon back in July 2019. Bill's beautiful wife Siobhán is never far from our thoughts and prayers. When we lose someone we love we must learn not to live without them, but to live with the love they left behind.

I have kept my final thank you for my wife Paula. Little did either of us know on that March night in 2015 when we first met that we would end up sharing this crazy, beautiful journey together. I prefer not to think about how my life might be today if we hadn't met. Thank you for taking my hand and never letting go. I love you.

When I retired from my radio career, I must admit I was quite worried about how I was going to fill the long days. Thankfully I am still very busy. I am currently writing another book, and I also present a weekly podcast diary for Senior Times: a meeting place for people who don't act their age. I think I may have found a new home!

You can listen to my podcasts at: https://seniortimes.ie/category/features/podcast-features/

My email address is garethocallaghan2021@gmail.com if ever you feel like writing to me.

You will find me on Twitter @GarethOCal and I am also active on Facebook: www.facebook.com/gareth.ocallaghan.1